This Constant Fight

Simon Russell

chipmunkapublishing
the mental health publisher

Simon Russell

Published by
Chipmunkapublishing
United Kingdom

http://www.chipmunkapublishing.com

Copyright © 2015 Simon Russell

ISBN   978-1-78382-218-8

About The Author

My first encounter with mental illness was over seventeen years ago in the spring of 1996. I was diagnosed with chronic depression and admitted to a private clinic in Windsor. Looking for a quick fix that would enable me to return to work I had a course of ECT treatment. I did return to work in 1998 and then begun a series of highs and lows that would later be diagnosed as Bipolar Affective Disorder. Between 2001 and 2010 I had five episodes of mania and was sectioned and hospitalised on four occasions. Two of the four periods of hospitalisation were in psychiatric intensive care units. I had the same number of chronic lows but these were treated in the community with medication and cognitive therapies. I do not regret having this illness as I now believe I can help others and leave a legacy.

Simon Russell

Chapter 1

It was spring of 2001. The telephone rang late one night. It was Maggie, the secretary to Victor Kiam, calling to tell me that Victor had died quietly in his sleep the night before in his apartment in New York.

The news was devastating. I had been with Victor when he had his heart attack in Switzerland. My family and his had spent a day together over Christmas a year earlier at his house in Florida. He was like a second dad and someone I admired and cared about greatly.

I put down the receiver and immediately recalled the evening before his heart attack in Lausanne. He had had a row with his wife, Ellen, and instead of joining Victor in Lausanne she had flown to Spain.

Victor was a great pragmatist and realist but that night I saw another side of him. It was almost as if he knew what was coming later that night because he was unusually reflective and sanguine. He told me that when the curtain came down he would be very happy and satisfied with his life.

He had enjoyed a great life with lots of business success and the trappings that came with success. More importantly he had a great family and that this was by far the most important thing in life.

He was also at great pains to tell me that he had always told the truth and that doing so was the single most important factor in being able to live the life that he wanted and had enjoyed.

There and then on the night of the phone call I decided that I too would live in the truth and that the next time my wife, Kim, asked me if I loved her I would be truthful and say no!

Our relationship had started to deteriorate some ten years earlier, just after the birth of our second son Joe, when Kim's parents asked her to leave the family office supplies company so that her brother could take it over.

Kim was understandably devastated as she had worked there for about ten years and apart from providing an income and a job that she enjoyed it put her in touch with her dad every day. He was someone that she shared a special relationship with and loved and adored in equal measure.

I also believe that Kim's parents nursed a rather old fashion view that a woman should be at home with her children.

Furthermore they knew I was a high earner and felt that Kim was adequately provided for by my income.

I wondered too if she was suffering with post-natal depression and suggested that she seek some help.

During those first early years of the 90's I was running the International business for a large American consumer products company, Clairol Appliances. The business was put up for sale and for two years or so I was consumed with the pressures of the disposal of the company that was under my responsibility.

I had to travel non-stop to the USA to meet with potential purchasers whilst at the same time visiting our subsidiaries around Europe and the rest of the world. I also had to deal with the day to day concerns of all my employees who during this period of uncertainty feared for their jobs.

Matters were not helped by the fact that the disposal was well publicised and I had to invest a great deal of time trying to keep our important customers loyal to us.

After a year or more of trying to sell the business our parent company, Bristol Myers, decided that they were not happy selling the business to the one and only interested party, Conair.

That being the case it was decided that myself and the rest of the management group in the USA and Europe could pursue a management buyout. The parent company told us that they would fully support us in this endeavour and lined us up with some banking options to purchase the company.

However at the last minute and despite the parent company's promises to us they accepted a last minute offer from Remington.

Devastated with this development and feeling thoroughly shafted I decided to take up an offer from Conair, a large American company in the same product field, who wanted to develop their business in Europe.

I got a signing on fee of £60,000 in cash and a salary of £125,000 per year plus the usual pension, health and motoring benefits.

Through the licensing of a global beauty brand and an acquisition of the French company, Babyliss, I built a business with over $50 million in sales between 1993 and 1996. However I was constantly tired and drained.

I felt like I had a backpack full of lead on me all the time.

Life at home was tough because Kim had not got over her removal from the family company and had not found another outlet for her time, skills and ability. She resented her parents and her brother and she was in a semi-permanent state of depression.

Because of the business pressures on me coupled with the exhausted state I found myself in I was not as supportive as I would otherwise have been. By the spring of 1996 I was at my wits end and had a breakdown.

My GP said that I was burnt out and needed to take time out. I was shocked. I had hoped that it would be something that a few pills could sort out. But no I was burnt out and required time out and a visit to a shrink.

I was also scared. I had two children at private school and a five bedroom house in Camberley with a big mortgage attached to it. I had a mental illness and feared that I would be seen as weak and useless for succumbing to it.

I felt suicidal and felt that ending my own life would be best for me and my family. I planned the wall that I would drive my car into when the time came. It was at the end of a long straight across Chobham Common on the road into Virginia Water.

I even managed to convince myself that I had Aids and had probably passed it onto my wife. I was utterly desperate!

The owner of the company, Lee Rizzuto, was on his way to the UK. We had some financial problems in the UK subsidiary caused within the UK arm of Babyliss. I was unable to reach Lee but left a message that it was necessary for me to take two weeks sick leave.

I was dismissed from my position!

With the way I was feeling my overwhelming reaction to being fired was initially one of great relief. I knew deep inside of me that something had broken and that it was going to be very difficult if not impossible to repair.

I sensed that whatever the future held it was unlikely to include the sort of business success and riches that I had already achieved.

I was unable to communicate this to Kim. I did not know how to put it into words and instead placated her with lies and deceit.

After a variety of tests and visits to a psychiatrist I was eventually admitted to the Cardinal Clinic in Windsor. I was fortunate in that I had private health cover and the Cardinal was more of a health farm than a hospital.

Kim resented my admission to the clinic and was reluctant to visit. The psychiatrist that admitted me later confessed to me that the reason he wanted me to become an inpatient was to protect me from Kim and her lack of understanding.

I was given a cocktail of antidepressants and lithium and engaged in group therapy and one to one Cognitive Behavioural Therapy.

The psychologist who worked with me on the CBT was extremely attractive and Kim insisted on being at all our sessions. This is of course rendered the therapy completely unhelpful because much of what I wanted to talk about was my failing relationship with my wife.

After two weeks I did not seem to be making any progress and whilst my own psychiatrist, Dr Hawthorne, was on holiday I requested a course of Electro Convulsive Therapy. I saw this as a quick and easy solution that would shock me back into life. I underestimated the headaches that followed the treatment and the long term convulsions that I still get from time to time.

When Dr Hawthorne returned from holiday he was surprised to learn of the treatment I had been given and told me that he would not have authorised it had been there. He knew that Kim was still working on me from afar and badgering me to man up and get back to work.

The treatment had some very short term benefit and I left the clinic in late September of 1996. I still felt terrible.

I had almost no energy and was unable to communicate effectively. I tried to hide this and took on and failed with some short term consultancy work. I had stopped socialising and playing golf. I just felt exhausted and spent a lot of time at home in a semi-comatose state.

I tried to tell Kim that I could not return to the type of work that I had done previously and that in my view we should consider using the equity we had in the house and my severance payment to buy a business that we could run together. We looked at some pubs and hotels but I knew her heart was not in it.

Finally something happened that from my perspective killed what was left of our relationship.

Kim came home one afternoon and announced to me that 'if I did not get better soon then she would go and fuck someone else!'

Simon Russell

Chapter 2

In the autumn of 1998 I finally managed to get back into permanent job. I had been told by an old acquaintance that Victor Kiam had invested in a struggling British company called Ronson PLC.

The business was a basket case that was set for multi-million pound losses due to the previous managements' overinflated view of the brand equity. They had purchased masses of stock in the male accessories markets including cigarette lighters, watches and pens amongst many other products.

They had also acquired two entrepreneurially run distribution channels in the duty free and mail order sectors and had made very significant promotional investments with the company's customers.

In short the product did not sell and the business hit the buffers with a mountain of debt, product being returned as it had not sold and a strategy that had clearly failed miserably.

The first job was to raise money through a rights issue to pay down debt and get the business on an even keel. With Victor as Chairman and his investment in the rights issue to back it up he and the rest of the team managed to raise the required cash to re-finance the company.

I made contact with Victor at his office in New York and offered my services to Ronson. He knew of me from the time some five years earlier when his Remington Company had purchased Clairol Appliances. We agreed to meet in a few weeks when he was in London.

We met at his suite at Claridges and within a couple of hours he had appointed me as Chief Marketing Officer with immediate effect. I was both relieved and excited and whilst I knew the business would be hard to rescue at least I had a permanent job and a regular income.

During the previous two years Kim and I had scraped through on a combination of consultancy income that I was able to generate and drawing down on a lump sum of about £68,000 that she had been given by her parents when they sold a property in Virginia Water.

Pretty soon after starting at Ronson I knew that major surgery was required on the business if anything was going to be saved.

I set about a product and distribution rationalisation program. I also made it clear to the board and key stakeholders that the business was about to get much smaller if it was to survive.

Whilst the news I imparted was met with horror the board had confidence in my judgment and ability and in a short time I became Managing Director with Victor as Chairman.

On the whole I felt well and was surprised at how easily I had jumped back into the saddle. I thought maybe that my breakdown was a one off and the future would be free from mental illness.

With the assistance of the other two directors we were able to restore the business, albeit with much lower revenues, to profitability.

Buoyed up by the rapid success I suggested to Kim that we move closer to the offices near Gatwick airport. Kim agreed and by moving further out of leafy Surrey we were able to get much better value for money in the housing market.

I also felt that the move might enable Kim to better get over the loss of her position in the family business and hopefully to find a new direction.

In late summer 1999 we moved to the beautiful village of West Chiltington in West Sussex. The village nestled at the foot of the South Downs and was about a half hour drive to my office and about twenty minutes over the downs to the sea at Worthing.

We bought a large five bedroom timber framed house set in the middle of its one acre plot. The gardens were totally secluded and we had an attractive outdoor pool.

Our eldest son, Sam, who was eleven, went to my old school, Seaford College, as day boy and Joe, who was seven, went to the local village primary school.

Life seemed to be good again. I had a good income, the children settled into their new schools and Kim saw her job as renovating the house that we had bought.

The relationship between Kim and myself was ok on the surface but underneath there was an uncomfortable lack of intimacy and love. Kim was not particularly interested in sex and I was not particularly interested in sex with her.

When we did have sex it, which was rare, it seemed to purely serve some form of carnal need.

We did not talk about important things and really just co-existed. We didn't or couldn't even bring ourselves to be friends. I think that my breakdown broke us as a couple and took all the joy and love out of our marriage.

Meanwhile the storm clouds were gathering at work.

Farzad Rastegar, who represented the largest shareholders that included Sir Jack Lyons, and who had suffered huge losses on his original investment wanted to take the business down a dot.com route whereas Victor, with whom I agreed, felt that we were better off sticking to the markets and distribution channels that we were already in.

I was truly piggy in the middle and tried many times to bridge the divide between them. I even took the Concorde flight to JFK one Father's Day to attend a meeting on the Monday between Victor and Farzad that I thought, wrongly as it happened, might get us all on the same page. I again travelled extensively in a bid to both try and harmonise a strategy and also to restore confidence in our business with our suppliers and distributors.

Kim hated me travelling all the time and would often not talk to me for weeks on end. She had started some renovation of the house and made friends with several of the other mums in the village. We both enjoyed living where we were but that could not compensate for the lack of love between us.

On one of my trips to the USA I was accompanied by Katherine, a marketing manager at Ronson. Katherine had recently separated from her boyfriend and on the flight over to New York we drank and laughed a great deal. We also kissed and had a fumbling but unsuccessful attempt at joining the mile high club. I was attracted to Katherine from the moment I joined Ronson. She was very petite, pretty and had a fabulous arse.

When we got to New York I was as high as a kite and ordered a stretch limo to take us from JFK to our hotel in Manhattan. Although I did not realise it at the time I was experiencing my first mild manic episode!

Simon Russell

Chapter 3

Katherine and I continued to have an affair almost to the end of my time with Ronson. We would often travel together and never lost the opportunity to indulge in the wonderful sexual relationship that we enjoyed. Occasionally I left home early and stopped at her flat en route to work for early morning sex.

As things turned out it was me who had fucked someone else!

I did have brief thoughts about talking to Katherine about us getting together but she was close to fifteen years younger than me and I could not visualise leaving my children for her. Had it just been Kim I would have done it in a flash!

At work the disagreement over business strategy continued at a pace and Farzad tried many times to get myself and the other two operational directors to come on board with his ideas.

I remained loyal to Victor and when the business shrunk to about £6 million it was obvious that the management team had to slim down.

I had started to get the familiar feelings of tiredness and was worried that I was heading for another breakdown.

Just before Christmas 2000 and after yet another angry exchange with Farzad I offered myself up for termination from the company. My offer was taken up and I left with six month's salary which equated to about £60,000 in cash. Certainly enough, providing my health stood up, to give me time to find another job.

The problem that I knew I had was breaking the news to Kim. I deliberately did not drip feed her information and left it until my termination package was agreed before telling her that I was once again without a job.

I took her out to dinner and towards the end of the meal I gently broke the news. She went ballistic and could not grasp that I really had no alternative.

I told her that I was outnumbered three to two on the board with my fellow operational directors siding with Farzad, leaving Victor and me out in the cold. ''Why you, why not John or Pam?'' she repeated and repeated. She just could not grasp the situation and was not pacified by the cash settlement.

I could not and did not tell her about the concerns I had for my health once again.

I understood Kim's concerns for the future and in particular for the children but we had in effect a year's money and by then a good stack of equity in our house.

Whilst I was tired I did not have the fatigue and exhaustion that plagued me before. I felt no need to see a doctor and was fairly confident, particularly having done a pretty decent job at Ronson, that I would find work fairly quickly.

Christmas of 2000 was a silent and morose occasion for Kim and me although we both separately tried to make it as much fun as possible for our two boys. Thankfully we had not booked our usual post-Christmas holiday to Florida or the Caribbean. That would have been awkward in the extreme with Kim neither talking nor looking at me.

After Christmas and the New Year I set myself two objectives. Firstly to get my name and CV out to the head hunters and secondly to put as much time as possible into the house renovation so that we could maximise the price should we end up having to sell.

Kim cancelled a course she was doing at college without explanation. I knew though that it was so she could keep her eye on me and ensure that I was doing everything possible to get a new job.

Reasonably quickly I found a very proactive head hunter who liked what he saw and read on my CV. He set about marketing me to the industry that I had largely been involved in for the majority of my career.

By the end of January he had got a bite on his line from the Wahl Clipper Company in the USA. They were looking for someone to manage their International business based in Sterling, Illinois.

The interview and selection process was rather long and tortuous but this was a family company with four third generation branches involved in the management and running of the organisation.

My first stop was to meet the UK managing director in Herne Bay, Kent. That went smoothly and the next step was to meet in Italy with Greg Wahl, the company president.

Around early Spring I was invited out to Sterling to see the manufacturing and marketing facility and to meet with members of the other branches of the family. As this job would involve re-location I insisted that Kim came along to look at housing and schools.

The four or five days we spent in Sterling were very successful. Kim liked the city and was taken to a school and shown a selection of houses in different price brackets.

At this stage we had not discussed salary but it was clear that providing my income was broadly similar our standard of living would be significantly higher.

I found all the Wahl family members to be very friendly and accommodating and although there was inevitably a bit of back biting I thought that I could be happy working in their environment.

Kim and I left Sterling with a warm feeling and we both said to each other that we felt that we could make it work. She pressed me at the airport before the flight and I got the feeling that she had already made her mind up.

Privately I was concerned on two counts.

Firstly, I was still extremely worried about our own personal relationship and felt reluctant about dragging her and the boys over to the USA where they would have no family support.

Secondly, I was worried about what would happen if I became depressed again and needed hospital treatment. The consequences of losing my job in a foreign country were somewhat mind boggling.

Prior to leaving Sterling, Greg Wahl made it clear to me that he and the rest of the family were favourable to my appointment. I agreed to think very hard about it and to get back in touch as soon as I had made my decision.

Little did I know what was just around the corner? Sleepy Sterling Illinois was the polar opposite of the journey I was about to take!

Simon Russell

Chapter 4

I fell madly in love with her the moment I opened the door.

It was shortly after we moved to West Chiltington that she appeared on our doorstep one wet and wintry day. She was bedraggled, dressed in a long wax jacket with matching hat. She had two very wet and dirty retrievers.

She told me that her name was Simone and she was a friend of Kim. She was one of the other mums at the local primary school in the village and had a son in the same class as Joe.

Her dishevelled state made her all the more attractive to me. She had a natural inner beauty and spoke like an angel. Kim was out and due to the state of the dogs she decided to wend her way home.

A few weeks later Kim arranged for Simone, her husband Rob and three children, Chantal, Rhys and Anais to come for Sunday lunch.

Over the table Simone caught me looking at her for what was obviously too long and I too found her doing the same thing to me. My danger antennae went up and I instinctively felt that this was a woman that I could finally leave Kim for.

I didn't know how or when. All I knew was that she was very much my type of woman.

She was petite, a size six to eight and had the perfect rounded and pert bum. More importantly she was truly feminine, obviously passionate, intelligent and funny and had the most gorgeous emerald green eyes that spoke volumes about her heart and soul.

Worried that I might be rumbled I spent the next couple of years being fairly unpleasant to Simone. I did not want to show my hand to her or to Kim. I needed to bide my time. It sounds calculating as I reflect on it now but it was just a natural path that I followed. Perhaps I am shallow and calculating man.

Kim would often ask me if I fancied Simone. My answer was always negative. I used to say that she was too headstrong and aggressive – qualities I secretly admired.

Kim and Simone became quite close friends and spent a good deal of time together. Rhys and Joe would often do sleepovers at one or other house.

Rob and I would go for drinks and played the odd game of golf together. We would meet for dinner every two or three weeks either just as a four or with other mutual friends we had in the village.

I was never really rude to Simone either directly to her or in front of others. I simply paid her little or no attention. I knew from Rob that she felt that I did not like her and I was not exactly over enthusiastic in refuting it.

On return from seeing Wahl in the US in the spring of 2001 I decided to pay Simone an unannounced visit. En route to London to see a consultancy client, Factory Design, I stopped by at her house. As luck would have it she was in the front porch examining the decrepit state of the ceiling.

If she was surprised to see me she certainly did not show it. She was very cool and invited me in for a cup of tea.

It was a beautiful sunny day and we sat out in the back garden. I apologised to Simone for being unpleasant to her since we had moved to the village and told her that I was angry with myself for not returning her warmth and welcoming hospitality.

I went on to say that contrary to her view that I did not like her that in fact the opposite was true and I was very fond of her. I talked a little about the situation with Kim and asked her to keep my visit confidential as Kim would react extremely negatively if she knew about it.

As I left I did not get the feeling that we were going to embark on an affair. I knew that I wanted to but I thought that she was happy in her relationship with Rob and she did not say anything to suggest otherwise. I simply thought that in the future we would become pals and I would not hide behind the silly mask of insincerity and obnoxiousness.

Soon after, Kim and I were invited to dinner with Simone and Rob. I don't know if Simone had told Rob about my visit. I suspect that she did as they had a very open and seemingly strong relationship.

After dinner we adjourned to the sitting room. Simone was curled up on one sofa with Rob and interestingly Kim and I were on the other sofa sitting at opposite ends. To me that told the story of the state of our respective relationships.

When the evening came to an end Simone insisted on driving us home as we had walked round earlier. We had quite a long driveway that swept up to the house. On being dropped off Kim went inside the house to sort out the babysitter and I went back down the drive to close the gates once Simone had driven out.

Simone waited by the gates and lowered her window. I put my head inside the car to say goodnight and give her a peck on the cheek. To my surprise and amazement I felt her warm tongue brush across my lips. As she sped off I felt like I had been hit by a lightning bolt!

Simon Russell

Chapter 5

I barely slept that night. I was on fire and fuelled with excitement and desire. Just one of the lightest, slightest touches had catapulted me into a love struck teenager.

I could not quite get my head around it. Earlier in the evening Simone was curled up in Rob's arms, apparently a picture of contentment and happiness. Was she showing me the type of lover she would be and expected me to be? My head was full of all the possibilities.

The following morning Simone called us and asked if we wanted to go to the seaside with the children to walk both of our pairs of dogs. We had a pair of German Shepherd sisters that were a bit unruly. We agreed and set off in our respective cars over the South Downs and into the beautiful village of Ferring.

After the walk we stopped at the Blue Bird Café right on the seafront. The café has been there since the 1930's and is a great spot with good food and seating outside and in. I went inside to get the drinks, leaving Kim, Simone and the five children and four dogs outside.

As I waited in the queue I felt her presence behind me. I looked round and there was Simone with a big and beautiful beaming smile that made me melt. I just wanted to wrap my arms around her and kiss her deeply and passionately.

Unfortunately the café has big picture windows and I could see Kim and the gang outside. We therefore had to be very discreet. I sort of blurted out a question about the night before. "Did what I think happen really happen" I mumbled.

Simone acknowledged that it had and it was both real and deliberate. By this time we were at the front of the queue and we needed to agree what if any next steps we were going to take. I suggested that we had an early morning dog walk the next day. Simone agreed and we arranged to meet about 7am the following morning.

We met as planned the next morning and walked, talked and kissed. When I kissed Simone it was so different to any previous kiss I had ever had. Even with Katherine the feeling I got was not as deep, powerful and overwhelming. From that moment I was hooked on Simone. She was a drug that I could not resist and a drug that made me high.

I learnt from Simone that she was unhappy in her relationship and that she was attracted to me too from our first meeting on that wet and windy day in the autumn of 1999. She wanted out from her marriage and she felt that free from the shackles of her marriage to Rob that the two of us had a future.

Despite the effect that she had on me I did suggest that we should take it slowly as we may just be two people that were helping each other out of bad relationships.

We met for our walks most morning s for the next week or so. Towards the end of May and about three weeks after our first walk Simone and Rob went on a business trip together for four or five days. Kim and I looked after Chantal and Rhys and as a thank you Simone gave me a cd from Dido called 'no angel'.

By that time I had agreed to work for Wahl as a consultant initially and had agreed a rate of £800 per day plus expenses. With the job sorted, my financial position secured and a start date in July I felt that the time was right, if I was going to do it, to be honest with Kim.

Whilst Simone was away the weather was beautiful and I set about painting the outside of our house. I had Dido playing at maximum volume and the words on the tracks all seemed to be telling me how Simone felt about me and our situation. It was particularly well chosen and I am sure deliberately so.

''What you feel is what I feel for you'' and ''I will always be alone if I am lying to you'' from Take My Hand and ''I want to thank you for giving me the best day of my life'' from Thank You coupled with the haunting melodies helped me overcome my sadness that she was away.

Although I did not realise at the time I was definitely high. I just thought that I was happy because perhaps I had found true love for the first time in my life. But no, I was intoxicated and it felt simply wonderful.

The morning after her return we resumed our early morning walks. Kim must have suspected something because she asked one day if I had enjoyed my walk with Simone. I told my last lie and said that I saw Simone at the end of her walk as I was just starting mine.

In addition to the walks we met several times during the day. We both wanted to go further than the passionate kisses and one day headed off for Brighton and got a room in a hotel. We had agreed that we would not have penetrative sex until we had both told our respective partners that we were leaving them.

We just about managed to stick to our agreement but came about as close to full sex as you can get. It did not really matter and did not spoil what was the most amazing sexual experience I had ever had. It was better than all my previous experiences put together. This was truly making love.

That first experience with Simone inspired me to write this poem about her a couple of years later:

Italian Girl

A vision of beauty, mind body and soul.
Infected by a freak, invaded her whole.
Confidence dented, but all invented.
Honest and sure, Heart so pure.
Filled with passion, up with the fashion.
Looks great whatever, feels even better.
Dimples in her cheek, illusion of meek.
Eyes of green, a lustrous sheen.
Fury and fire, never too far.
Fatal attraction, a constant distraction.
Engaged in love, a gift from above.
Completely at one, until it is done.
Saved a life, despite her own strife.
A giver for life, a wonderful wife.

Afterwards we went for a late lunch at Browns in The Lanes in Brighton. During lunch we hatched our plan.

We had decided that we would not do it simultaneously. At that stage all we knew was that we had a very strong attraction for each other. We had not talked about living together and I had been clear with Simone that maybe we were just helping each other out of our respective relationships.

We agreed that we were not going to site our relationship as the reason for wanting to separate. We had not consummated our relationship and whilst we both knew that we would we did not want to complicate things with Rob and Kim.

The following week we executed our plan.

Chapter 6

Simone told Rob first. I suspect that he knew it was coming as he apparently reacted fairly unemotionally and they told their children immediately.

News travelled fast and Kim went to see Simone as soon as she heard of their separation. Kim was as surprised as I was. She too had seen Simone and Rob as a rock solid couple and she had said to me that she envied the way that Rob doted on Simone.

A night or two later, the moment that I had been waiting for since that fateful phone call from Maggie came. Kim and I were having dinner on the patio and we were talking about the situation with Simone and Rob. She asked me if I loved her and I told her that I didn't and hadn't for the last ten years.

She was shocked. I had expected her to immediately get angry but that didn't come for an hour or so later. I felt terrible about what I was doing because even though I did not love Kim anymore I really did not want to hurt her. She had been through a tough time herself and really didn't deserve another hit, particularly one as life changing as this.

When she did eventually get angry she told me that I was sick and I didn't know what I was saying. I was able to tell her that I did not need to put up with her histrionics and anger anymore. It was her anger that was one of the major reasons that I did not love her. I went to bed.

Our bedroom was downstairs and for several hours I could hear on the phone. Ironically she was speaking to Simone. She burst into the bedroom and told me to get up and "fucking talk to her". I told her that we had nothing to discuss and that my mind was made up. I went up to the spare room and left her talking once again to Simone.

The next morning I took the boys to school and when I returned Kim was spoiling for a fight again. I felt liberated because I knew I did not have to fight with her anymore. I once again told her that my mind was made up and there was no going back.

In our case we decided at that stage not to tell the boys. It was something that I was dreading and did not know how I was going to do it. Kim, whilst very angry and upset still nursed the belief that I was sick and would come to my senses. In a way she was right. I was high, not psychotically at that stage but definitely too high to be making the sort of decisions that I was making.

For the next few days I slept in the spare room and was in touch with Simone. Neither Rob nor Kim had connected the dots between Simone and me at that stage. Simone and I planned our next moves the first of which was to now consummate our relationship.

The following Saturday Simone had a wedding to go to on her own and told Rob that she was staying over with her sister. I told Kim that I was going to be away that night and did not need to justify myself in any way. She was at this stage playing things quite coolly, convinced that things would work out for the best.

She repeatedly told me to get help for my obvious illness and I should have taken her advice. I didn't because I was intoxicated by Simone and did not want any help from anyone. Mania, as I later found out to my enormous cost, is such an amazing feeling it is practically impossible without sectioning for anyone to help.

That Saturday when Simone was at the wedding I drove to my parent's house to break the news to them. Every day that spring and summer seemed to be warm and sunny and we sat out in their garden in Purley. They were not surprised, or at least did not show it. Neither of them, they admitted had really liked Kim and my dad said that the whole family were surprised when I married her.

I remember feeling very anxious and stressed at the time. My heart was racing. My speech was very rapid. My driving was erratic. I was more or less chain smoking and I was drinking quite heavily. All signs I would later come to recognise as symptoms of my manic episodes. I should have been hospitalised and given powerful anti-psychotic medication.

I left my parents and spent the afternoon preparing for the night I had been waiting for with Simone.

Chapter 7

I drove back towards West Sussex. Simone's wedding was close to Crawley and I decided that Horsham would be a good spot to explore.

After some searching I found a beautiful five star hotel, called South Lodge, in Lower Beeding, Just outside of Horsham. I booked the Ronnie Corbett suite which was set on two floors with the bathroom up a small flight of stairs. I stopped in Horsham and bought a boom box and fresh copy of Dido's 'no angel'.

The hotel is situated in beautiful grounds and I walked around for a couple of hours to while away the time until Simone was due to arrive in the early evening. I also drank and smoked heavily to try and calm my anxiety and stress. Strangely when I am high I can consume very large amounts of alcohol without getting drunk. In the depressed phase I don't touch alcohol and smoke four or five cigarettes a day.

Simone arrived around seven and looked stunning in her wedding attire. She was full of beans and like me excited and high about the night ahead. It was the culmination of the five or six weeks since we had taken our first walk together.

She loved the suite and being a very witty and funny person herself found the fact that it was named after Ronnie Corbett appropriate and apt. We had a glass of champagne and toasted our achievement. Simone then had a bath and I sat with her chatting, stroking and washing her and filling our glasses.

After her bath we ordered room service and had dinner in the room. The sun had started to go down and a beautiful sunset was emerging in the distance.

After dinner I put the Dido cd on the boom box and we embraced and kissed and started to make love. Before I entered her, Simone asked me if I was sure that I wanted to go ahead with this and all that came with it. I was in no doubt and thrust into her. It was simply so amazing and special and we made a connection deep inside her that I had never felt with anyone else before or since. It was as if my penis found an inner cave that was a perfect fit and only I could enter.

During our love making Simone scratched my back raw. It was as if she was marking her territory so that I could not go back on my promise to leave Kim and be with her. She also exclaimed "mine, mine" at one point as if she had won this enormous battle. This troubled and worried me as it seemed overzealous but she was an extremely passionate person who lived life to the full. She also had Italian blood in her and with it came a fiery personality.

We made love all night and were still exploring and searching each other when the sun came up the next morning. We both came many times simultaneously and it was obvious that we were compatible sexually. We didn't sleep and finally had to tear ourselves apart from each other around nine. We bathed together and had breakfast before we headed off back to West Chiltington and our respective homes.

Chapter 8

I hadn't slept and was as high as a kite. Whenever I am sleep deprived I have an ability to take myself up to try and cope with the side effects. I suffered terribly with jet lag and this ability, as dangerous as it was, was particularly helpful in my travels to Asia, Australia and the USA.

When I got back Kim and the boys were in good spirits and again it was a beautiful sunny and warm day. Joe was about to head off to a friend's house and I told Kim that the time had come to tell the boys of my decision. She vehemently did not want this and did her utmost to try and persuade me not to go through with it. I wish that I had listened to her.

Without doubt it was the most heart wrenching, destructive and hurtful thing that I could possibly do. Both boys collapsed in tears and were uncontrollable. Kim told them it was my decision and she did not agree with it. She told them I was ill and when I was better this would not happen.

They were nine and thirteen for Christ sakes. What sort of fucking bastard does that to his own children? Had I been well enough and able enough to foresee the damage I was doing I would not have gone through with it. Yes I knew Kim and I were not forever but I had always vowed I would not leave her until the boys were old enough to cope with the separation.

That night Sam came and slept in my room. I was sick, stupid and irresponsible and should have called it off there and then. But I didn't and for that all four of us paid a very high price.

The next morning I took the boys to school and returned home readying myself for the storm that was to follow. I told Kim that I was serious about leaving her and that I was not ill. She flew into a rage and just repeated her view that I was ill.

That night I went to stay with my sister, Jenny, in Lingfield. She too was having marital problems and I went over to try and help her. My driving was again very erratic and I barely made it. My heart was racing and my driving followed the same pattern. I would accelerate and break continuously. When I arrived in Lingfield I went to the local pub and had several large vodkas to try and calm my nerves and reduce my stress.

That night with Jenny I was not helpful at all. She was upset and stressed and my mania was the last she thing she needed. I left early the following morning still highly stressed and more manic than ever. I drove erratically back to West Chiltington and up to the top of the South Downs.

I had convinced myself that my father was not really my father and in fact it was my Uncle Terry who was my father. I called Jenny and told her that this was my belief and the reasons for why I knew it to be true. It was obviously complete rubbish but I could not be told otherwise. She was very worried for me and told me to go home and see a doctor.

I went home and Kim greeted me fondly. I also told her what I had discovered about who my dad really was. She could tell that I was a mess and suggested that I had a bath to try and calm down and that she would call the doctor. I said yes to the bath and no to the doctor. At that moment I almost changed my mind about leaving Kim but the bath did calm me a little and I was ready again to re-state my position to her.

After the bath I told Kim that she should call her parents and let them know that we were separating. She refused to do so and told me to do it.

Later that morning I called her dad and told him the news. Strangely he didn't ask how Kim was and simply said that I had spoiled his day. Like Kim I think he was in shock and really did not see this coming.

When it finally dawned on Kim that this was for real and there was no negotiation to be had she started hyper-ventilating and I got really worried about her. I tried to calm her down and asked if I should call the doctor. Rather than the doctor she asked me to call a friend in the village, John Hodge, who we were quite close to. He had some experience in mental health and despite being unwell himself with M.E. he kindly agreed to come round.

After some time the three of us decided it would be best if Kim's mum and dad came over and took her home to Virginia Water with them for a few days. I made the call to Kim's parents and they agreed to the plan. I decided it would be best if I was not at the house when they arrived and John agreed to stay until they had been and gone.

Whilst I was waiting for Kim and her parents to leave the house I went to the local pub and again necked several Vodkas to try and reduce my stress level which had started climbing again. I called my dad and told him that I knew he was not my father but that it was ok and that he had done a great job. He was obviously baffled but very calmly said to me "that did I mean that Uncle Terry was my spiritual father?" I later wrote a poem that is included in my 'Hole in my Soul' book called 'Spiritual Father'.

I was so high and completely psychotic. I needed help but would not accept it from any quarter. Eventually I called Simone and told her too about my paternal discovery. Fortunately she did not take flight and came and got me from the pub.

She took me home, upstairs to her bedroom and undressed me. She kissed me, sucked me and brought me down gently and finally lifted her dress and rode the stress out of me. It worked as well as any anti-psychotic drug and within a couple of hours I was able to leave her and pick Joe up from school.

Over the next couple of days I was able to look after the boys. The weather remained good and after school we swam and one night we had some of their friends over for a bar-b-q. I was trying to keep things as normal as possible.

On the third day I got a call from Kim to tell me that she was coming back the following day with her parents and they were going to stay over until we had resolved matters. They would be back in time to pick Sam and Joe up from school. My stress level immediately went up and I decided that I would not be there when they returned.

That night after the boys had gone to bed I set about preparing for my departure. I put together everything I would need for a permanent separation as I could not see myself returning and going through the stress ceiling again.

After doing the school run the next morning I loaded my car with all I thought that I needed. Most importantly of all were the things that would enable me to be completely free from Kim. I took my Passport, credit cards and other personal documentation together with a selection of clothes, both business and casual. For some reason I even took my mountain bike!

Over the next couple of days I stayed in local hotels and then booked a beautiful cottage for a week at Duncton Mill, a specialist fishing lodge, with its own pool. Remarkably the weather remained good and Simone and I spent the week lounging round the pool and making love.

One evening Kim brought Joe over to see and stay with me. She did not know that Simone and I were seeing each other but when Joe was there Simone brought a take away and the three of us had dinner together. I told him that Simone and I were just friends. The next morning I took Joe back to West Chiltington and dropped him back with Kim and her parents.

As soon as I approached the village in the car I felt my stress level going through the roof and could not cope with the physical manifestations. Joe must have told Kim that Simone was there the night before because later that day she called me to tell me that "I was a fucking bastard who was fucking her best friend!". Furthermore "I could give up any fucking hope of seeing my fucking children again!"

Simone and I discussed Kim's reaction and we decided that she could not stop me seeing the children however much she felt betrayed by both of us. By comparison Rob and her maintained decorum and put the feelings and welfare of their children first. By then Rob knew that Simone was seeing me and had as much right to be angry as Kim. However he was just not an angry kind of man.

The following day I went back to see the boys after school and as I entered the house I was confronted by Kim's mother wielding a broom and waving it me. She reminded me of the wicked witch of the east. She told me to get out and that I was not welcome. My stress level yet again was sky high and not wanting to make a bad situation worse I left the house for the last time.

Chapter 9

By now it was early July and I was due to start working with Wahl in a few weeks' time. At the time I was also working with a pal on developing a range of kitchen electrical products under the Gary Rhodes brand. I needed to get myself set up with a permanent address and a new bank account.

After a short stay in a little cottage in the garden of a large house in Midhurst, which had no mobile phone reception, I moved into a small three bedroom character farm cottage in Graffham.

It was called Peter's Farm House and it was perfect in that the main bedroom, with an en suite, was up one set of stairs and the remaining two up a separate set. There was a small kitchen with a dining area and utility room off to one side, a downstairs bathroom, a fabulous sitting room with a huge log fireplace and a separate office with its own entrance.

The house was set in the middle of its third of an acre gardens and the property sat amongst farmland and stables. It was truly idyllic and a perfect set up for Simone and I to enjoy and for the boys to stay when they wanted.

By this stage Kim's parents had returned home and we had started to speak again. I am not sure if it was because she wanted me back or that she did not want to come second to Simone. I would like to the think the former but suspect the latter.

Nevertheless I was able to see the boys occasionally and on my birthday in the middle of July she paid me visit with a birthday card. She had a good snoop around the house and could see that Simone had not moved in and I guess she believed all was not lost. She brought Sam with her that day and he and I played golf at Cowdray Park. I think that was the last I saw of him or Joe for about three years.

Shortly after my birthday I was to tell Kim that Simone and I had in fact taken our friendship to a new level and there was no going back. She asked if I was going to marry Simone and I replied that I didn't know but probably yes. That sealed my fate and ultimately I think, albeit sometime later, the fate of Simone and my relationship. Kim did win that battle in the end!

With war established between us it was even more important that I became entirely independent of her. I approached Barclays Bank and they set me up with two accounts with combined overdraft limits of about £25,000 and a credit card with at least a £10,000 credit limit. This was on the back of my consultancy agreement with Wahl and was unsecured on anything. Money was easy to come by in those heady days.

In addition to the Barclays line of credit I got myself an assortment of other credit cards, which in addition to the ones that I already had gave me somewhere in the region of £50,000 - £60,000 of open spending power.

The farm house had a monthly rental cost of £1500 plus bills and I the house in West Chiltington had a £300,000 mortgage at a monthly cost of close to £2000. I was not unduly concerned at this stage because at £800 a day from Wahl I thought that running two houses was affordable. It was, all the time I was working twenty days a month at £800 and I did not consider that this might change.

I also did not figure that my high mood would lead me to trade in my BMW for a Porsche Carrera 4 with a monthly cost of £1000 , nor buy a boat on the river at Beaulieu for £15,000 or live a millionaires lifestyle for two or three months with regular weekends at the Master Builders Hotel in Bucklers Hard.

Simone and I eat out almost every night we were together, mostly at The Halfway Bridge just outside Midhurst where we had become friendly with brothers, Simon and James Hawkins, who owned the pub with their mother.

Simone at this stage was still living in West Chiltington with her children and at weekends left them with Rob so we could spend time together. Rob was very accommodating and looked after the children at every opportunity. However he quite sensibly refused to move out of his own house, sleeping on the sofa when Simone was there and in their former marital bed when Simone was with me. Simone didn't like this but she could not have it all ways up!

Throughout this period I was high, definitely had delusions of grandeur but was not psychotic. I was just about in control but my expenditure was ridiculously out of control. Simone and I were having a blast though and I did not want that to come to a stop.

In early August I went for my first trip to Wahl in Sterling. It was a familiarisation trip essentially and I met with all the departments and had a tour of the production facility. I also had prepared a presentation that was an outsider's perspective on Wahl which highlighted their strengths, weaknesses, opportunities and threats. I delivered the presentation to several groups and it was well received by all.

I met with the four sets of male cousins that were involved in different aspects of the business. I also had the opportunity to meet with the board of directors as they had a meeting already scheduled during my time there.

By the end of the week I had agreed with Greg Wahl, my boss, what I would work on in the coming three weeks and set a return date in Sterling for the end of August. In broad terms I was to go on a fact finding mission around the different subsidiary companies and distributors in Europe.

On my return Simone met me at the airport and was dressed like a chauffeur – a little insight into her sense of humour. Thereafter for the next two or three weeks I was back at work. I was away several nights a week and Simone and I would spend as much time as we could together. Weekends were largely spent at Bucklers Hard, on the boat during the day and in a Master Builders Hotel Suite at night.

I was a complete nightmare on the boat. I had no experience of sailing and even though it was a motor boat I was fine in a straight line with no wind or tide. Anyway we managed largely accident free and spent a lot of time on our mooring in the middle of the Beaulieu River just making love, drinking and sun bathing. It was such a joyous time and as soon as I was on the water any stress just melted away.

During this period I had been approached by the Assistant District Attorney for New York who was investigating the tax affairs of Lee Rizzuto. To put it in perspective Conair now has revenues of over $2 billion annually and Lee Rizzuto is the sole proprietor.

I was asked if I would co-operate with their investigations whilst making it quite clear that I had no choice in the matter. I said that I would on the proviso that they confirmed in writing that I was not a subject of their investigations, which they duly did. I agreed to meet with the Assistant D.A. and his colleagues on my next trip to the USA at the end of August.

Whilst I had nothing to hide from the US authorities I was slightly nervous about giving evidence against Lee. Rumour had it that he had mafia connections which being of Italian origins and self-made was not as farfetched as it might sound. Also paranoia, at least in my case, accompanies a heightened state.

I decided that it would be best if I had someone with me when I was interviewed. I considered having some legal representation and knew a lawyer in Chicago who I thought might represent me. In the end I decided that having a lawyer would probably arouse more suspicion than provide protection and asked Simone if she would join me.

The next trip was a ten day session with a weekend in between. Simone and I worked out that she would come over the weekend and I would set up the meeting with the authorities for the Monday evening in Sterling. As a measure of the importance that they took this assignment, the Assistant D.A. and his team were flying from New York to Chicago and driving two hours out to Sterling.

I knew that I had some information that they would find interesting. Soon after joining Conair in the spring of 1993 Lee visited me in the UK with his girlfriend, Denise Jansen. He had travelled to Heathrow from Lugano and when I dropped him and Denise off at their hotel in London he gave me a small carrier bag with the £60,000 joining fee in it in £50 notes.

I was worried!

Chapter 10

At the same time as this was going on Simone was becoming increasingly frustrated with Rob. She wanted him out of the house but he refused to leave. I was also concerned about what life would be like if Simone and Kim remained in the same village with children at the same school.

I then made my second biggest mistake. I suggested to Simone that her and her children should come and live with me in Graffham. I was not seeing my own children and this was making me increasingly depressed. I would cry often and Simone was very comforting.

She was also very annoyed with Kim and encouraged me to either force my way back into their lives or go through the courts and CAFCAS to ensure that I saw them again. She knew that my not seeing the boys posed a very real risk to our own happiness and future together.

I was fond of Simone's children and thought that having them live with us would somehow compensate me for not seeing my own. I had forgotten that three's a crowd and that other people's children seem to bicker and fight much more than your own.

Simone jumped at the opportunity as this clearly bound us together and solved a big housing and living problem for her. There was an empty four bedroom modern build house in the same lane as the farm house and I agreed that we could all move in together. The rent on this house was £2000 per month plus bills so I was increasing my outgoings which on this house and the one in West Chiltington were now in excess of £5000 per month.

I sorted the move out with the letting agent. It was quite smooth going because both properties were owned by the same landlord. It was agreed that the move would take place during the first week that I was away in Sterling and before Simone came out to join me. In addition to my belongings (I had spent about £10,000 on furnishings for the farm house) Simone would bring all the furniture and belongings that she needed from her house in West Chiltington.

A third and very significant event happened that August. I was made aware that there was an opening for a managing director at Remington's UK business. With there now being no chance of me relocating to Sterling I decided that this opportunity was worth pursuing.

I made contact with Neil DeFeo, the president of the company, who as luck would have it was over in the UK at the time. Due to the megalomaniac activities of the previous managing director who by then had been fired, the business was set for heavy losses in the year and was substantially dragging down the performance of the company worldwide.

I felt that I was a good fit because I had both industry experiences with Clairol and Conair together with a good turnaround record at Ronson.

I was informed that Neil was staying at the Sir Christopher Wren Hotel in Windsor. I left a message for him and he quickly got back in touch. That same week we met for breakfast and chatted generally about my past and what I was doing at the time. Neil was impressed with my credentials and told me that he would think about how to take my application forward.

An old friend and ex-colleague of mine, Paul Martin, had been promoted to the position of managing director but Neil felt that it was not working out and change was not happening fast enough. Neil had to figure out a way forward that would be the least disruptive. He also wanted me to go through a series of interviews with key people in the organisation – who were all based in the USA at that time.

One of these people, the Chief Financial Officer, also happened to be in the UK at that time and it was arranged so that I met him for breakfast at his hotel in Woking. We met and chatted about the difficulties in the UK business and my suitability to provide a fix. Afterwards I drove him to the Remington office in Staines. Two down about five more to go!

The next agreed step was for me to meet with Victor Kiam's son, Tory, who I knew from the time we had been with Victor in Florida at Christmas several years earlier. Tory was a main board director with a fiduciary responsibility at Remington. He was scheduled to be in the UK in the second week of September and a meeting was set up for us.

I headed off as planned to Sterling in the third week of August. I was up front with Greg Wahl and told him that Kim and I had now separated but that did not necessarily affect my position with the company. Although I did not believe it, I said that in certain respects a move was made more possible by my change in circumstances.

I could not afford to lose my job with Wahl at that time and Greg bought my story. We also had not discussed my remuneration if I was to make a move to Sterling but it was clear that paying me at my market rate in the UK would mean breaking with their salary scales. Only Greg would be paid more than me which obviously created all sorts of issues. This also helped me to buy some time.

I spent the week working with my new colleagues on the international issues and had my first meetings with my direct reports. By the end of the week I had settled into the position and gained the respect and trust of my colleagues. I had meetings with the marketing and new product teams and discussed ways in which to take the International business forward. The main thrust of what we wanted to achieve was greater harmonisation of product and pricing across the European markets.

On Friday I had arranged for a limo to pick Simone up from O'Hare airport in Chicago and to bring her to The Paddle Wheel Inn in Oregon, Illinois. It was about a half hour drive from Sterling but was in a beautiful location on the banks of the Rock River. I had booked a river view suite and I rushed over there after work at five o'clock.

When I got there she was already checked in and I raced along the corridor to our room desperate to see her again. I felt so in love with her and every moment apart felt like a lifetime. She opened the door and leapt into my arms. I ordered a bottle of Bollinger and a Pizza and we confined ourselves to our quarters for the night and most of the next day.

Late the following afternoon we headed off to Sterling because we had been invited to dinner with Greg's brother, Mark, who had a lovely house on the river. We spent the evening on Jet Ski's messing about on the river.

Mark was a great guy but was regarded, somewhat unfairly in my view, as the black sheep of the family. He ran the Pet Care division of the company which was a relatively small but growing sector of the business.

I seem to recall that the overall company turnover was in the region of $200 million and the Pet Care division was probably 10% to 15%. The numbers were a bit vague as it was a privately held company and certain confidential details were restricted to me as I was not a full time employee and had not signed any confidentiality agreements.

On the Sunday Mark had invited us to go sky diving on the outskirts of Chicago. I think that he wanted to test my mettle as it was not something I had done before. The closest I had come was parascending! I reluctantly agreed on the basis that I would be attached to Mark or an instructor on the way down.

On the Sunday morning Simone was feeling a bit jet lagged and I got cold feet about the sky diving. We also just wanted to hang out together by the pool and not have to think or do anything apart from what we did together. I called Mark and politely declined the offer.

The following morning I drove to work in Sterling and left Simone to explore the surroundings. We had an important night ahead of us with the meeting with the Assistant D.A. and his team scheduled for six pm. I told Greg about the meeting and he was happy for me to go early.

He, like most of the personal care appliance brands in the US, was not keen on Conair because of their aggressive sales and marketing policies. Conair were also very aggressive in their sourcing, had a brilliant team in Hong Kong and were just very slick at what they did. Conair's success was down to Lee Rizzuto's personal drive, ambition and commitment. Business was everything to him and he surrounded himself with similarly likeminded and talented people.

I got back to the Paddle Wheel around five so that Simone and I could plan our strategy for the meeting. It was also important that she eased the stress out of me before what was going to be a heavy session. We fucked quickly and urgently, showered and both got dressed in smart suits.

We were ready!

Chapter 11

The call came to the room. Our visitors had arrived and were waiting outside the hotel by the river. Because we had a river view suite we could go out on to the balcony to scope our foe. It was like 'All the Presidents Men'. The three men were all in dark, sharp suits and look liked an FBI squad.

We went down, were greeted very politely and they offered to take us for dinner. The Assistant D.A. asked most of the questions. Another of the team members had a recording device and I was asked to 'tell the truth, the whole truth and nothing but the truth'.

I explained that Simone was there in an advisory capacity and that she was not a lawyer. I told them that I had considered legal representation but because I had nothing to hide I did not think it necessary.

Over dinner I was bombarded with questions. Most of them were to do with people and procedures. They named a variety of characters most of which I had not heard of. They asked me if I knew Denise Jansen to which I replied that I did and I elaborated by telling them about the times that Denise had been with Lee in my company and what sort of relationship they had.

I had stayed with Lee at his house in Greenwich, Connecticut and Denise was there overnight. It was clear, despite Lee once introducing her as a marketing manager at a meeting with Boots in Nottingham, that they had an intimate relationship.

I liked Denise. I also really felt for her because living with Lee must have been a nightmare. I noticed that she had scars on her wrists and had clearly had some issues in the past. She was always very pleasant and friendly to me and she made a good contrast to Lee who tended to be overbearing and intimidating.

By this time Lee had left Denise and ironically had left her for a good friend of Denise who happened to work at Conair. Denise was not best pleased and therefore when the Assistant D.A called with the IRS I imagine that she had no problem in being truthful and expansive.

Over dinner I was told by the Assistant D.A. what crime they were pursuing Lee for. Apparently, between 1989 and 1998, he had directed two companies to falsely inflate the service fees they charged Conair and they had given him over $3 million in cash which was paid into a bank account in Switzerland.

They also asked me about our transactions with suppliers and our accounting procedures. I was able to be clear on this because ultimately we only had one product supplier, Conair Hong Kong, and therefore if there was any 'creaming off' from the suppliers it was done there.

Our accounting procedures and IT were set up by the Conair US and we simply complied with corporate policy. We were audited by a large accounting firm and we complied with local UK rules and regulations.

As far as I was concerned I was clean and had nothing to hide. Except one thing and I was waiting for the killer question. My stress level was pretty high and I had to take several bathroom breaks. Simone often stepped in and reminded them that I had had a breakdown and she was not going to let me have another.

Finally the question came. '' Did I receive £60,000 in cash from Lee on his arrival with Denise Jansen from Lugano in 1993?''.

I was in a tricky situation because I knew that Denise would have almost certainly told the truth. In the end I decided to tell a lie! I was stressed, high and verging on paranoia and was worried that telling the truth would come back to haunt me.

I told them that I had received ECT treatment in 1996, it had affected my memory and I could not recall any such payment.

Lee pleaded guilty in April the following year and was ordered to personally pay $2 million and for Conair to pay $3.6 million to the IRS. He also got a three to four year jail sentence.

I did feel that some poetic justice had taken place for both sacking me when I was ill and for dumping Denise for her friend.

The meeting concluded and Simone and I had a bottle of champagne and toasted our achievement of getting through the ordeal more or less unscathed. I was so glad that Simone had been with me. I don't think I would have held up quite so well had I been on my own.

With that business concluded I then spent a couple more days working at Wahl and again agreed with Greg the next steps in my assignment. I was to continue my work with the European subsidiaries, arrange a conference in the UK to which he would attend and finally to return to Sterling around the end of September for a conference of the Asian agents, subsidiaries and distributors.

Simone and I returned to the UK overnight on the Wednesday and the next major challenge awaited me!

Simon Russell

Chapter 12

When I got back to Graffham the new house was up and running. Simone had brought her furniture over and the house looked and felt great. All the children had their own rooms and we had a lovely bedroom with views over the South Downs.

Downstairs we had a large kitchen and utility room, a well-proportioned dining room and two sitting rooms. The house was set in about an acre of gardens which were mostly laid to lawn. It was a great set up and one that I thought would accommodate all of our needs very well.

Simone had also set up schooling for Chantal and Rhys in Petworth and Anais in the local village primary school.

Soon after our return from the US the children and dogs moved in and we were a family. I was away on business for most of the first two weeks in September and therefore was immunised somewhat from the day to day stresses of family life.

On the morning of September 11th 2001 I met Tory Kiam in London for breakfast to discuss my application for the job in the UK with Remington. Tory was already a supporter of mine as his dad had always reported very well on my skills, loyalty and ability when I was at Ronson. We discussed the situation in the UK and my suitability to the role.

Tory was very positive and felt that I was a good fit and would report back accordingly to Neil DeFeo. Tory was due to fly back to the US that day and for some strange reason or premonition I said that if his plans should change to let me know and perhaps we could have dinner.

On my way back I called into Factory Design in West London. They were working on the Gary Rhodes project that I was involved with.

Just after 2pm as I was driving home Simone called me on my mobile. I could tell she was tense and she asked me if I had heard the news. I hadn't as I had been in meetings and the last thing I expected was for her to tell me that the twin towers had been attacked. She gave me a running commentary and told me that they had collapsed.

I immediately called Tory on his mobile to offer my condolences and thoughts. He was obviously in shock and was watching the same news feeds. He was particularly worried for his family and friends. He told me that his investment vehicle had an interest in the Windows on the World restaurant at the top of the North Tower. The North Tower was the first to be hit and the last to be destroyed.

By now it was clear that all flights had been cancelled and the US airports had been locked down. I repeated my offer of dinner and told him to call me if I could do anything to help.

When I got home I immediately emailed Greg Wahl and offered my condolences and support. I also said that I was sure that the UK would stand together as one with the US over this terrible incident. Little did I know that Tony Blair would take us into Iraq and allow George Bush to subjugate our democracy in his ill-informed and stupid assault on that country? I was so incensed I later wrote two poems about these pair of clowns:

The Burning Bush

A soul so black, burnt and charred; a mind so twisted heartless and hard;

A brain so empty, ignorant and dumb; a heart so dry, emotionless and numb;

How on earth is our earth in his hands? No intelligence, no knowledge of foreign lands;

A simpleton with hunger to make his mark; No more dangerous combination, none so stark;

In cahoots with terrorists in the Arab states; lining his pockets from his wealthy mates;

His only determination to protect the oil; without a care of the damage to foreign soil;

He feigns his sorrow at the body bags; just pawns in his game, just metal tags;

His disquiet and discomfort easy to see; covered with bluster, bullshit and glee;

To a nation naïve and self-absorbed; his reign protected, his reputation not daubed;

But to the rest of the planet he is evil to the core; unless you profit from poverty and war;

Whoever is next they surely cannot be worse; than Bush the devil, immoral and perverse.

The Great Pretender

He will be remembered as the great teller of lie, darkness, deceit and warmongering cries;

He came to power on a tide of glory, no opposition to counter his pious story;

The US model was his claim to fame, riddled with corruption, the corporate game;

How we were fooled by his evil stare, and the constant chants of 'vote for Blair';

He repaid his backers with honours galore, high powered jobs, titles and more;

But his only interest was self-preservation, remembered as the saviour of the nation;

And to prepare for his later luminary career, buying new friendships year after year;

His lasting legacy, the war in Iraq, with Bush the dog and Blair the bark;

This cosy relationship immoral and black, throughout the turmoil he dodged the flack;

The blood of many indelibly printed, his soul won't suffer, his medal already minted;

David Kelly's death ordered to cover his sin, he knew too much and NO votes could win;

His followers bizarrely aped his every word, like lambs to the slaughter, a characterless herd;

It's ironic his initials are the same as a foul disease, how many has he killed in his attempts to appease;

Yes of course he is the great pretender; for the worst PM he is the best contender.

(All poems in this book taken from Hole in my Soul and published by Chipmunkapublishing.com)

The rest of September I worked on Wahl business. I continued with my travels to the various subsidiaries and worked on the harmonisation program that I had agreed with the Greg in Sterling.

I also had lunch with Neil DeFeo and in essence he confirmed his continued interest in me and wanted me to fly to New York and meet with a few of his direct reports, particularly those on the marketing and product development side of the business. I suggested that I did this over a weekend when I was next with Wahl at the end of September. Neil agreed that this was a good idea and acceptable to him.

I felt like I was making progress on my application with Remington but I didn't at that stage really consider the reality of going back to a £125,000 per annum salary. After tax this would net me in the region of £6,000 per month and my housing costs alone were in the region of £5,000. However I wanted a permanent job and I was not sure how much longer Wahl would keep me on without me making a move to Sterling. I also reckoned that if I did move to Sterling that at best I would get in the region of $125,000 per annum. Not enough to fund two families!

For the time being though I was billing about twenty days a month at £800 per day so despite my massive outgoings things were affordable.

Emotionally life was getting tougher and tougher for me. The autumn had started and throughout my life it is a time of year that sets my depression triggers off. Simone and I were not getting away as much at the weekends and we were spending every other weekend with her children. Contrary to what I thought and despite their warm and loving feelings for me they were making me miss my own children even more. Tears flowed more often and Simone was finding it increasingly difficult to console me.

Coming off the high and being below my median mood I was not the same Simon that Simone had had got into bed with. I felt tired and less able to maintain the marathon love making sessions she relished. I was also less doting on her and I think that this led her to seek attention elsewhere.

We were at the Halfway Bridge at least three or four times a week including almost every Sunday lunchtime. The Sunday sessions would last many hours as we had become friendly with a local antique dealer, David Sowden who was as crazy as hell. He drank heavily and was addicted to weed. He had a lovely girlfriend, Jenny, but treated her like shit.

The brothers who ran the pub really knew how to appeal to Simone and certainly did show her the attention that she craved. James was a fairly plain and laid back character but his brother Simon rated himself as the local lothario. Had I not been so down I would have intervened but by this stage the depression I was incurring gave me a devil may care attitude.

I should have taken some action because Simon Hawkins would come back to haunt me in a major way!

Simon Russell

Chapter 13

At the end of September I headed back to Sterling for what would be the last time. I spent the weekdays working with the Asian distributors and on the Friday night I went to Chicago to attend a trade show with Mark Wahl and to be near the airport for my flight the following morning to New York.

The Saturday morning was a beautiful bright clear day and the plane approached La Guardia from the south side of Manhattan, right over the Statue of Liberty. I looked out and could see the empty space where the Twin Towers had been. It was like looking at some one really famous without their two front teeth!

I was picked up at the airport by a driver and taken up to Greenwich, Connecticut. That afternoon I met with Lester Lee, the head of sales and Tim Simone, the head of product sourcing and development together with several other key people in Neil's team. That night Neil and his wife, Sandy, took me out to dinner. I was not on the best form and certainly more subdued than Neil would have seen me previously. I think I had passed the final test though!

I returned to Chicago on the Sunday afternoon and rather than drive to Sterling that night I decided to try and cheer myself up by staying at The House of Blues Hotel in the city. It is a great place to stay if you are a music lover like me. To further try and relieve my growing depression and annoyance at Simone I ordered in a therapeutic massage with a hand job as an extra.

I felt marginally better and relieved afterwards and had a good night listening to live music in the show bar. After Florence, Chicago is my second favourite city and I had enjoyed some great times there over the previous ten years or so.

The following morning I drove myself out to Sterling and the final showdown, I hoped, with Greg. That morning I could sense tension in Greg and I knew he wanted me to 'piss in the pot or get off'. I was able to bring things to a head by calling Neil and asking him for a decision. He verbally and by email confirmed my appointment as Managing Director of Remington UK with effect from November 1st. The salary was, as I suspected, £125,000 per annum plus a bonus potential of 30%, a car allowance, pension contributions and a phantom equity share scheme.

I then told Greg of my decision to accept The Remington job. He was upset but I think he was relieved at the same time because it meant that he did not have to tackle the thorny issue of salary. I hope that I gave value for money to Wahl for the short time I was there. They are a great family company with excellent products and strong ethics.

I took the rest of October off and Simone and I went to Barbados in the last week prior to my joining Remington. For the first six days we had a great time and re-ignited the flames that we had enjoyed at the start of our relationship. We had a beautiful ground floor apartment right on the beach at St James.

We spent most of the week lounging on the beach, swimming, supping Pina Coladas and making love. We had a lot of fun and laughed a great deal. We also hired a car and saw some of the tourist spots and drove over to the rugged Atlantic coast. I have been to Barbados three times and it is a magical Island.

However on the last night I was consumed by depression. I could not communicate with Simone and felt physically and mentally drained. We had dinner in a fabulous restaurant but 'whilst my lights were on I was not home'. It was a frightening feeling and reminded me of the breakdown and depression I had experienced in 1996.

I was dreading returning home and living a domesticated life with Simone and her children. I was consumed with sadness about not seeing my own children and I was not at all looking forward to starting the job with Remington. I no longer felt up to the challenge. The dawning of the financial situation was also starting to kick in.

We returned home overnight on the last Thursday in October and on arrival back in Graffham, I did a quick turnaround and headed for the Remington offices in Staines where I was due to meet Neil DeFeo, who himself had flown overnight from New York.

I was jet lagged, exhausted and depressed. Fortunately I did not have to do much that day apart from to be there alongside Neil when he told the troops about my appointment.

We had a group meeting and one to one meetings with the department heads. The most difficult meeting was with my old friend, Paul Martin, who as a result of my appointment was being demoted to Sales Director.

I managed to survive that first day by the skin of my teeth. If people had looked very closely they would have spotted my stress signs – shaky hands, gulping of fluids, a croaky voice and a time lag from question to answer. Maybe they did spot them and just put it down to jet lag as they knew I had flown in from holiday that morning.

The weekend was a living nightmare. I just wanted to sleep and try and get myself into some sort of shape for the Monday morning. Simone wanted to party and insisted on Sunday lunch at the Halfway Bridge. To make matters worse Simon and James invited us out on the Sunday night to commemorate their father's death.

I should have put my foot down and said no, or at the very least not gone myself, but I took the path of least resistance and Simone and I went along. We got back around midnight and she was a little high and excited and wanted sex and lots of it. It was obvious that she had got off on Simon's flirting with her and probably imagined that it was him who was fucking her!

Monday came too quickly and I had to get up at six am in order to shower, dress and make the two hour drive to Staines for nine am. I didn't want to be late but was. The M25 was a nightmare and solid from the A3 to the Staines exit. By the time I got there I was even more depressed and frustrated at the prospect of having to do this most days of the week. I was also really pissed off with Simone about the night before.

I entered the building and went up to my office on the top floor and hid in there trying to look at reports and emails. I was completely useless and frankly achieved nothing that day or any other day in the first two months that I was there. The first eight weeks of any appointment are invariably the most critical and I achieved zip!

I was fortunate in that the business was in a mess and the projections continued to get worse. The business was heavily Christmas dependent and the sales forecast kept slipping. This meant that everyone was running around like headless chickens and for the most part my lack of activity was not shown up.

I did manage to venture out of the office one day to see Argos, one of the company's largest customers. I stayed over the night before with another old friend, John Bell, who was the Argos account manager. Simone had told me that she was seeing an old friend for dinner that night. When I called her about seven it turned out that the old friend had cancelled and instead she was going out to dinner with Simon Hawkins.

I was dumbfounded and shattered when she told me. I saw it as a deliberate attempt to get under my skin by both of them. Maybe I should not have been surprised because I was depressed and not giving Simone what she needed. I tried calling her a couple of times later in the evening but she did not pick up. I called the babysitter around eleven pm and she was still not home.

I was enraged. I wanted to kick her and her children out of the house I was struggling to pay for. I wanted to remind her of the words on the Dido song '' I will always be alone if I am lying to you''. I wanted her to understand what it was like to not see your own children and the other sacrifices that I had made for her. She of course had made sacrifices for me too but I didn't consider this at the time.

I couldn't sleep that night and was phased out at the meeting with Argos the following day. John said to me afterwards that I was very quiet and withdrawn.

In short I was very unwell and struggling to cope with being alive. I knew I needed help and I knew that I would have to seek it soon before everything collapsed around me.

Little did I know how bad it was going to get.

Chapter 14

On the way back from seeing Argos I stopped in at the Halfway Bridge. I didn't know what I was going to say to Simon and in the end rather than getting angry with him I made it clear that I loved Simone and nothing was going to get in my way. Actually I think I came across very weakly and probably just made the situation worse.

Rather than getting cross with Simone I just fucked and fucked and fucked her that night. She even said to me that she should obviously go out with Simon more often if this was going to be my response. Again I was very weak. I should have tackled her head on but did not have the energy or words to try and confront her.

I just about scraped through, personally and professionally, until the Christmas break. I stupidly thought that a week or so off might enable me to re-charge my batteries and go back in the New Year with renewed vigour and energy.

Christmas was hell on earth. I could not cope with the loss of my children at this time of year. I was not placated or consoled by having Simone's children with me. I sadly had started to resent them.

On Christmas Day we went to a local pub in Midhurst with Simone's sister, Jacqueline and her partner Steve together with the three children. Simon Hawkins and his brother James were also there. I didn't want to be there and hung in the background without saying much to anyone. Simone looked very sexy and flirted hard with the Hawkins brothers.

On the way back to the house Simone received a couple of text messages one of which was a flashing Christmas tree. This brought much merriment to the children.

When we got back to the house Simone was on fire and dragged me upstairs for sex, leaving the children downstairs with her sister. Once again I knew something had happened between her and Simon Hawkins. I duly obliged as best as I could in my wholly knackered state but again wondered who she was thinking about as we fucked.

Later in the day Anais asked me if I would show her the flashing Christmas tree again. I got Simone's phone, showed the Christmas tree to Anais and then checked out the other message. To my horror it was also from Simon Hawkins and simply said 'I could have eaten you today'. I was mortified, angry and distraught. I couldn't confront Simone until her sister had gone and the children had gone to bed.

Later, when I did confront her, she was very defensive and embarrassed and just passed it off as Simon being Simon. I just about summoned up the strength to tell her that it had really pissed me off and that if we were stay together we would not be able to go to the Halfway Bridge or socialise with Simon or James again.

She pleaded with me not to take it so seriously. She said that her entire social life revolved around the Halfway Bridge and the people there and by cutting it off I was in turn cutting off what she considered to be her only friends. We were due to go there on New Year's Eve and I said that this was no longer possible.

The next morning Simone took the children to Rob who was then looking after them for a few days. She was gone a very long time and clearly did more than drop the children off. Whilst she was gone I considered my options and felt that the only course of action for me to take was to ask Simone to leave the house and return to West Chiltington.

When she returned she was very apologetic and tried to explain it away as a terrible mistake and mix up. I reminded her of the previous dinner date with Simon and the high state she was in when we got back from the pub the previous day. I asked her who she was thinking about when we had sex on Christmas Day! I really backed her into a corner but stopped short of asking her to leave.

By this stage I was really worried because I recognised that my mental state and the physical manifestations was as bad, if not worse, than when I had ECT treatment some five years earlier. I knew I was mid breakdown and in need of rapid intervention.

Later that Boxing Day we went to my parents for a late lunch. I was silent throughout the meal and my mum knew there was something wrong. After lunch I went into the lounge and lay on the sofa. A little while later Simone came in and lay with me. We stayed the night and headed back to Graffham the next morning.

The rest of that Christmas period is a blur and I have no real recollection of what happened or what we did. I was exhausted and I guess spent a lot of time once again in a semi-comatose state.

The day before New Year's Eve Simone pleaded with me for us to go to the party the following night at the Halfway Bridge. I stupidly relented and agreed to go. On reflection I should have let her go on her own and kicked her out on New Year's Day if indeed she did go.

For me it was an awful night. It had a school days theme and I was dressed up like Just William. I had no fight left in me. I was punch drunk. Simone was in her element and danced and flirted the night away. I felt the constant presence of Simon Hawkins like a leech on my skin. We had been given a room in the pub for the night and I finally managed to drag Simone to bed at about four am.

I barely got any sleep that night. I had so much shit going through my head. The next day I was wrecked but at Simone's insistence we made a return visit to the pub for a long lunch and a dissection of the night before. I sound very weak for not putting my foot down and stopping this ridiculous situation but I was simply too unwell.

My idea for a restful Christmas could hardly have been more wrong. I went back to work on the second of January in a worse state than when I left in December. I turned on my computer at work and could not read any of the print. After several frightening panic attacks and vomiting in the toilet, I made the decision to go home and rest.

I didn't go straight home. I was suicidal. I drove down to a car park by the river in Pulborough and considered how best to end my life. I was in the car for a couple of hours and eventually phoned my mother and told her what was going on. She told me to go home to Simone and get a doctor's appointment as soon as possible.

Simone greeted me with surprise and concern. She knew I was in trouble and as a result she was in trouble herself. I called the surgery and got an emergency appointment the next morning.

When I saw the doctor he diagnosed my problem immediately as chronic depression and said that I should take some time off and he would get me an appointment with a psychiatrist as soon as possible. He also gave me some anti-depressants and sleeping pills. I asked him how I could explain it to my employer and he told me to tell them that it was a stress reaction.

That afternoon I emailed Neil DeFeo and told him the news. I fully expected to be sacked!

Chapter 15

I remained suicidal and several times disappeared in my car with all my pills determined to end the torture that I had to endure. Simone had me out every morning with her walking the dogs. I could barely put one foot in front of the other. The way I felt is summed up in another of my poems from Hole in my Soul.

Lost

Where am I now, I'm totally lost, chilled to the bone, cold as frost.
I entered the maze some time ago, impenetrable walls, no directional flow.
In so deep, there is no way back, no light in sight, just very dark black.
I am not sure how I ventured in, looking for something, perhaps new love to win.
I have been inside such a terribly long time, my life before forgotten, so sublime.
No sense of a future without an exit route, I pray for a gun and someone to shoot.
I often feel dizzy, totally out of sorts, a ship in the ocean without any ports.
Where are the signs, recognition wiped clean, no benchmarks around, nothing to glean.
Hopelessly, helplessly, haplessly estranged, heading nowhere, worryingly deranged.
Running out of energy, little fuel in the tank, no one to blame, only myself to thank.
Hoping still for a miracle to occur, that might save my soul and the inevitable defer.

A miracle did occur in the form of a psychiatrist, Dr Jean Sherrington. Simone and I went to see her at the Centurion Mental Health unit in Chichester around the middle of January 2002. She agreed with my GP that I was suffering with chronic depression and prescribed a new dose of a different anti-depressant. At that stage she did not feel it necessary for me to be hospitalised but would see me regularly.

She also told me not to expect too much too soon as the medication often took four to six weeks to take effect. She recommended that stayed off work for the foreseeable future. The appointment was actually in a mental health ward and was very scary. Consequently I was delighted not to be admitted.

I brought Neil DeFeo up to speed with the developments and got the IT team at Remington to set me up at home with access to the in house systems. Neil was not best pleased but in fairness to him he was very supportive. We spoke on the phone a few times and he tried to encourage me as much as possible. He had scheduled a visit to the UK for the early part of February and wanted me back for that time. He made it clear that that was as far as his generous spirit would stretch.

Simone too was supportive. She no longer felt the need to drag me off to the pub and continued to get me walking as much as possible. The weekend before Neil's arrival we went down to Devon to stay with another of her sisters, Pauline. Simone is the youngest of thirteen children and therefore has plenty of siblings dotted around the country!

We had a really relaxing and pleasant time. The house was set up high with great views across the moors. Being winter it was very wet and windy but we still walked a lot and had good food and good relaxed company.

We drove back on the Sunday night and on the Tuesday I returned to work feeling a little bit brighter. I caught up with everyone as best as I could and at least showed my direct reports that I was alive.

Neil arrived the following day and we spent the rest of the week reviewing progress and establishing how the turnaround was going. We also had a budget review session on the Saturday morning. Considering my state of mind I performed adequately and I think he could see that I was on the mend.

Before leaving he told me that there was a board meeting in New York at the end of the month and he wanted me there and to present the UK budget and forecast to the board.

I got to the meeting in New York and survived the board meeting. I was on auto-pilot but the lights had definitely started to flicker on. I called Simone after the meeting and told her that it had been a success and headed back to the airport and home.

By this time my financial situation had caught up with me and I had to make some changes. I had already traded in my Porsche for a less costly Mercedes estate. We moved houses to a less costly house in Midhurst. I phoned Kim and I told her that I could no longer afford Sam's private school fees and she had to sell the house in West Chiltington. Remarkably she took the news reasonably well. I suspect that she knew that I was unwell again as she too was being treated by Dr Sherrington.

By the spring I was well on my way to recovery and probably operating at fifty percent of my capacity as compared to zero to ten percent at the worst of the attack. I was starting to direct operations at work and starting to have a real impact.

In the middle of April I hosted a two day conference for my direct reports in Midhurst. They all stayed at the Halfway Bridge which was now somewhere Simone and I frequented again. An easy truce had been established between Simon and James and me. At the conference we agreed the remaining tasks to be tackled to fully repair the business and everyone's agendas were set. We also took some time out for a game of golf at Cowdray Park.

By May I was really 'cooking on gas' and although I didn't realise it at the time it was the start of another high. I saw my role now at Remington as leading from the front, seeing customers and driving the business forward. It looked like that at the very least we would make several million pounds of profit compared to a horrendous loss the year before.

I particularly felt that the shaving and grooming side of the business needed a dynamic injection. The product range was great and the pricing was competitive. We were the only shaver brand to have both a foil and a rotary offering. The possible solution came in the form of a suggestion from our PR agency.

They had dealings with an up and coming hairdresser, Adee Phelan, who claimed to have cut David Beckham's hair. A meeting was quickly arranged and there began another crazy journey!

Simon Russell

Chapter 16

I met Adee at the Dover Street wine bar in central London. A restaurant and live music venue, predominately jazz, with a great atmosphere. We immediately struck a chord and chatted into the night about the possibilities of working together. He told me that he had cut David Beckham's hair but was not regarded as his official hair dresser.

Furthermore he knew and worked with Maria-Louise Featherstone who was Victoria Beckham's makeup artist and close friend. A plan formed in my head that involved Adee as our professional support for PR and events and if remotely possible and affordable David Beckham as the new face of Remington shaving and grooming products.

Adee and I chatted for most of the night and he came back to my hotel and we smoked his skunk together. He was pretty wild back then and I know he has cleaned up his act since. The last thing a manic depressive should take is any form of recreational drug especially in the heightened phase of their illness. However, I had not been diagnosed with manic depression at that time and indulged with will.

That night we also hired an escort each. He was disappointed with his but mine was amazing. So much so that she stayed and chatted with Adee when he came up to my room later. She wanted to know what happened and why he had had such a bad experience. She also suggested to him that he call and ask for her next time.

The following morning which was a Friday, I drove Adee to his home and place of business, which at the time was his flat, and waited while he fulfilled a couple of bookings. We then drove to Staines where I introduced him to my marketing director, Richard Rietjens. Richard listened to Adee and agreed that the plan was very well worth pursuing.

I then took Adee home to Midhurst and put him up at the Halfway Bridge. We had some drinks there and Simone joined us. We ended up at some friends, Peter and Suzie, who lived in Graffham, who had invited some other folk from the pub. I was pretty exhausted and in the late evening Simone and I left Adee there amongst new friends and went home to bed.

That weekend I had arranged a boy's trip with Jeremy Martell, my financial advisor and another friend Peter who was an old squash and golfing buddy, down to the boat on the Beaulieu River. The plan was to take the boat along the coast to Lymington and stay the night at the Rhinefield House Hotel in the New Forest.

On the Saturday morning I picked up Adee from the Halfway Bridge and set off for Beaulieu. The weather was perfect and by then I had traded in my fuddy duddy Mercedes for a beautiful black Jaguar XK8. Why wouldn't I? I was well again and had the world at my feet! I was however dangerously high. Not psychotic at that stage, that would come later.

We rendezvoused with Jeremy and Peter at the Beaulieu slip road off the M27 and headed for the boat. The boat was moored in the middle of the river so Peter and I rowed out to it with the aim of then driving it back to collect Adee and Jeremy from the shore. I started the boat and as I drove off the mooring line got stuck round the propeller and we were well and truly stuck. The boat was a wooden Sandbank sea cruiser built in 1959 and fully restored a couple of years previously.

Fortunately a short time later another motor boat came cruising towards us. It was piloted by an ex conservative party MP called Chris Hawkins. He quickly assessed the situation and threw us a rope. He then towed us round in circles so that the mooring rope untangled from the propeller. We then picked up Adee and Jeremy and set sail for Lymington with Chris alongside us.

We stopped at Bucklers Hard and picked up a couple of escort girls who had agreed to spend the afternoon and night with us. Not quite the boy's only weekend that was billed. When we got to Lymington Jeremy got cold feet about the whole deal and decided after a couple of drinks at a local bar, Fat Cats, he returned home.

Adee, Peter and I had a great evening and I met up with some guys from an events company in Lymington who I was planning to use for a team building conference in the middle of June. Around ten Adee and Peter and the girls went back to the hotel in a taxi and I stayed on for another couple of hours. I felt really well, on top of the world and strong again.

I got back to the hotel around midnight and went in search of the boys and girls. As I entered the corridor that Adee's room was in there was an overpowering stench of Skunk and an audible din of two people having sex.

I knocked on the door and Adee opened up still naked and with a condom on his penis. The girl he was with, known to me only as T, I had known for a while. She had a bronzed body, blonde hair and was very fit and very enthusiastic about her work. She told me previously that her and her husband used to get off on the stories she told about her work!

I don't like the smell of Skunk and decided it was best to leave them to their business. I went in search of Peter and the other girl, who I think I had met on one occasion. They too were happy with each other so I decided to go to my room and get some much needed sleep.

The next morning I took the girls back to their car at Bucklers Hard. After some lunch in Lymington we all returned home and I put Adee on a train back to London. You could say that he and I had got to know each other pretty well by that early stage of meeting each other.

In order to try and advance the David Beckham deal I called a friend, Barry McGovern who was best buddies with David Gill at Manchester United. Barry got details of Beckham's agent and acting as an intermediary consultant approached them with the offer of talks with us.

Around the same time Simone and I went for a short break to Siena in Italy. Her full name was Simone Pontet-Piccolomini. The Piccolomini dynasty go back to 13th century Siena and have an amazing estate with letting cottages a few miles outside of Siena. We stayed in a wonderful old farmhouse with its own secluded pool.

When we went into Siena we learnt of the Palio which is the bareback horserace around the outskirts of the central square, Il Campo. The race was taking place in the first week of July and the third week of August and I decided it would be a great event to take our two largest customers, Boots and Argos. The Piccolomini Estate Manager was very helpful and told us he could make all the arrangements from there including ringside seats on the balcony of a restaurant.

When we got back I asked Paul Martin if he would like to go ahead with this for the race in early July. He was very positive and I handed him all the details to follow up on.

On our return from Siena, Simone and I went down to Lymington as I was renting a three bedroom flat overlooking the harbour. I wanted a bolt hole down there as it was too cold and damp to sleep on the boat and I wanted somewhere of my own to try and entice my children down to. I was able to afford this because by this stage, Rob was contributing to the housing costs in Midhurst.

It was far from sensible though and I spent about £8,000 on furnishings. My expenditure was dangerously out of control again and I was running out of credit!

Chapter 17

I had a lot of balls in the air by now.

The core Remington business was looking strong. We had taken steps to improve our margin by eliminating low margin products and the exchange rate with the dollar was lowering all our product costs. Paul had done a great job of disposing of our redundant inventory and this in turn was helping to get our warehousing and distribution costs back to acceptable levels. Declan Mullane, my director of operations had also made substantial cost savings by getting a lot of the rework done at source in China. If the sales held up as expected we were set fair to smash our profit target and end the year with maximum bonuses.

The conference at the Master Builders in Bucklers Hard was set for the middle of June and I had created teams made up of four or five people from different departments in the organisation.

Barry was charged with getting a deal on the table with the Beckhams. I had not at this stage shared this with Neil DeFeo because I wanted to see if it was doable first. Paul and Richard were right behind me on it and felt it would be a real coup if I could pull it off.

Paul was organising the Palio and had got agreement from Boots and Argos to attend. I had invited Neil to this with his wife and he had jumped at the opportunity. He was also going to attend the conference.

Richard was working on an agreement with Adee and had already booked him and Maria-Louise Featherstone to do a demonstration at the conference.

Charged with mania I was floating round keeping all the balls spinning.

On the personal front my divorce from Kim was finally going through and I had to attend court in Reading on one occasion to try and resolve the distribution of assets and access to the children. The judge ordered us to talk at least once a week about the children which we both duly signed up to do.

The first phone call one Sunday night was to be the one and only. I phoned Kim at the allotted time and instead of discussing the boys she just ranted and raved on about what a bastard I had been. I didn't bother after that. Mediation was not going to work either.

Kim was asking for all the equity in the house, the cashable investments and a slug of my pensions. We later agreed a full final settlement that essentially left me with my pensions and a small amount of cash to pay off my legal bills. With what she had Kim had enough to buy a three or four bedroom property locally whilst also paying off the outstanding overdraft to Nat West who held our joint account.

The final judgement was made in my absence in early July. I was poor but I was finally free from Kim and the housing commitment in West Chiltington.

Throughout this period I was regularly smoking weed which just served to fuel my mania rather than calm me down. I liked the feeling though and did not consider the side effects. I was clearly unwell and this was demonstrated by the crazy number of initiatives that I had on the go at one time. I should have just let the business do what it was going to do that year, restore the profitability and take the £35,000 or so bonus. But my illness drove me on.

In the first week in June I had to go to a conference in Mystic, Connecticut. I was flying out on the third of June which was the first of the two day jubilee bank holiday. On the Sunday Simone did something at the Halfway Bridge that set me at odds with Simon Hawkins once again. I was mad with him and mad with her.

On the Monday Simone drove me to the airport but we were late and I missed my flight. That in itself was not a major problem due to the frequency of flights to New York but I had to reschedule my driver the other end. I was stressed to hell and it was getting to the danger level. Because I had an hour or two to wait, Simone and I went back to the car, drove it up to the roof and had a quick screw.

When I got to New York I felt terrible. I was too high and the stress was seeping out of my pores. I got the driver to drop me off at a bar in Stamford rather than take me to the drab country club hotel I was booked into in Greenwich. After a few too many drinks I checked into a cheap hotel around the corner from the bar. That night, fired up with mania and anger, I had a procession of four separate escorts visit me at the hotel.

By the following morning when I was picked up by a driver I had not slept for over thirty hours and was a physical and mental wreck. I was driven to the Remington offices and after a short meeting with Neil to discuss the conference in the UK and the Palio I made my excuses and asked to be driven up to the conference venue in Mystic.

I got up to the hotel and was given a beautiful suite overlooking the ocean. I desperately needed to sleep but couldn't. I had not slept for close to forty eight hours by this stage and was completely dead on my feet.

I made a complete idiot of myself over the course of the conference. It was attended by all the senior management from around the world and in many cases it was the first time that I had met them.

My mania had now reached a mild psychosis and I had become delusional.

I decided that I could challenge Neil for the presidency of the company. I had a three point plan that would at least double the revenues and triple the profitability.

Point one was to acquire and integrate the Wahl Clipper company.

Point two was re-launch the power blade which was a battery powered vibrating wet shaver that delivered the closest shave of any other device.

Point three was to hire the Beckhams to be the face of the brand worldwide. Victoria would represent our female hair care and beauty products and David our shaving and grooming products.

I tried at every opportunity to thrust this idea forward and get buy in from my colleagues. Neil got frustrated with me and wanted me to stay with the agenda as set. I was continuously disrespectful towards him and made a fool of myself.

At one point we had an agent for a corporate motivational company deliver a presentation to us. He compared the owner of his company to Ghandi. That was like red rag to a bull to me and I tore into him. I was asked to leave the room by Neil. After he was gone everyone agreed that this was not the company that we should be using but without exception were highly critical of the way that I treated the poor fellow. I argued that we did not need an outside organisation and I could undertake what was required myself. I did not make many friends that week!

By the end of the conference Neil was very upset with me and understandably so. Before leaving he instructed me to take the following week off work and to try and restore some perspective and equilibrium.

I had arranged after the conference to get the train up to Boston to meet briefly with Tory Kiam. I got there later than planned and only had about a half hour slot before I had to head off to the airport. I told Tory of my plan for the business and that I would like to challenge Neil for the presidency of the company.

I think he was glad that I only had half an hour and was glad to see the back of me!

I flew back to Heathrow and on the flight acted like a multi-millionaire. I was in business class and drank copious amounts of alcohol. I was the life and soul of the party for the stewardesses or so I thought. I bought a load of gifts from the trolley and handed than out to the stewardesses to thank them for looking after me so well. I don't think that they knew what hit them!

As I landed back on British soil I thought that the future was very bright. Little did I know that within four weeks my job with Remington would be terminated and my career in the consumer products industry brought to an end!

Chapter 18

Simone picked me up from the airport as that day we had agreed to go to the opening of Adee's salon in Southend.

After Simone picked me up we went to the Runnymede Hotel, where I had a corporate membership, to swim, shower and change. We then went to Greens in Sunningdale to get me a trendy outfit for the salon opening.

Simone drove us to Southend and after a couple of drinks and a tour of the new salon we made our excuses and left. We drove down to Lymington because I wanted to spend some time on the boat de-stressing and we also needed to finalise the details of the conference with the events company down there.

Both objectives were achieved but I did one extraordinary thing. I bought a gun! It was only a gas powered repeating air pistol but none-the-less a dangerous tool in the wrong hands. By this stage mine were definitely the wrong hands! Apart from the delusions I was experiencing, paranoia had also started to set in and I wanted the gun for protection.

We sorted the details of the conference with Steve from the events company. It was going to be a three day affair with the delegates arriving on the Sunday morning. It was going to be a mixture of product demonstrations, business presentations and team building exercises. Entertainment came in the form of a live band on the Sunday night and dinner at Fat Cats in Lymington on the Monday night.

We took over all the rooms at the Master Builders in Bucklers Hard for the event. Prior to the conference on the Sunday we booked an extra couple of nights so that we could entertain Adee and Maria-Louise Featherstone. I wanted to make a good impression with Maria-Louise in particular so we got a good report back to the Beckhams. We also wanted to finalise Adee's contract.

The stage was set and I was happy with the arrangements.

I did not take the following week off as instructed by Neil. I needed to keep the balls spinning so that I could bring the various separate initiatives together into one marvellous symphony. I wanted to tie things up with Beckhams in time to inform Boots and Argos about the news during our trip to Siena for the Palio.

Barry told me that the Beckhams had considered our approach and were keen to take things further. The outline of the agreement from their side was that in return for £1 million a year that we could have a combined worldwide package with Victoria working on the hair and beauty products and David on the shaving and grooming products.

Our UK marketing budget was north of £5 million so it was affordable in the UK alone. Outside of the UK and in markets like Spain and Italy the Remington brand was barely known and we did not sell any shavers. With David Beckham on side our brand image and awareness would sky rocket. To me it was a no brainer. A meeting was set up with Victoria in London on the Tuesday morning of the conference and Richard, Neil and I would attend.

Towards the end of the week prior to the conference, Adee, Maria-Louise and her boyfriend, a model, Richard and I descended on the New Forest and the Master Builders Hotel. We agreed what form the demonstration would take with Adee on stage doing a hair clipper demonstration on Richard and Maria-Louise's boyfriend. Maria-Louise would do the makeup for the show.

We also spent plenty of time partying. I had stretch limos to take us everywhere. We went to a live music event at Lymington Yacht Club on the Saturday lunchtime. Saturday night I had booked a large and beautiful motor cruiser to take us across to the Isle of Wight for dinner. Unfortunately on the way back it lost its navigation systems as we were approaching the Beaulieu River. We had to be rescued by the lifeboat and were towed back to Ryde on the Isle of Wight. We spent an unexpected night on the boat which all things considered was not too uncomfortable. I made sure that Maria-Louise had the captain's cabin but we were all able to sleep in relative comfort.

We returned unscathed on the Sunday morning and met with Adee to finalise his contract. I think we agreed to pay him in the region of £10,000 per month for the first year and he would act as our professional spokesman and demonstrator for PR purposes. I signed the contract. Adee was happy and it meant that we could introduce him to the delegates of the conference when they assembled for dinner that night.

The conference started around 3pm and we kicked it off with an African Drum exercise that got everyone to eventually harmonise. Dinner was on a beautiful motor yacht and Richard did a brilliant job in introducing Adee to the thirty or so delegates. We cruised to Southampton and once there we boarded a larger boat for a live music event. I had booked a band called Some like It Hot who I had first seen at the Dover Street Wine Bar. They were a really upbeat swing and jazz ensemble with a great lead singer.

Some of the more adventurous delegates got into the mood but for the most part it was damp squib. Simone, who was there as organiser and photographer, certainly got into the mood. We were smoking weed and at one point she dragged me off to an empty room, stripped off and got me to fuck her.

The following morning Adee did his demonstration which went down well with all. By this time Neil had arrived. In the afternoon the delegates went off to do the team building exercise and I took Neil, who is a great car enthusiast, to the Beaulieu Motor Museum. I told him about the proposal with the Beckhams and he was luke warm but agreed to come to the meeting with Victoria the following day.

That night we had dinner in Fat Cats in Lymington and a group of about twelve of us stayed late and had a ball. I was still very high but less stressed and the psychosis had eased.

Richard and I left on the Tuesday morning to go to London for the meeting with Victoria. Neil left separately because he had some TV interviews to do relating to a court case that we had won against Philips. This win enabled us to sell our rotary shavers in competition to their previously monopolistic position on this technology.

Richard and I met Barry in our hotel and ran through the details again. Barry was not going to attend the meeting. Richard and I got suited and booted and headed off for our meeting, which I seem to recall was in the Tottenham Court Road.

We were shown into an office and Victoria and a colleague were already there. David was away at the World Cup in Japan and Korea and Victoria was several months pregnant. I was immediately struck by her beauty. I was also impressed by the handle she had on what was required of them to successfully promote our products. At one point she said "we could sell shit loads of this stuff in America". She really made a huge impression on me. She was witty, bright and incredibly intelligent.

Richard and I talked through some of the products and their potential. She loved what we had to offer. She also commented on how well we had looked after Maria-Louise. I was pleased that my strategy had worked!

Neil arrived about an hour late and the first thing he said was that he had not heard of her or her husband. My heart went into my mouth and thought immediately that he had killed the deal. What a wanker!

In the taxi back he told me that if we paid enough money we could have Tiger Woods and that the Beckhams were a silly idea. He had no vision.

We went to dinner and celebrated our victory over Philips and he made it clear that he did not want us to pursue this deal with the Beckhams.

This was great news for David and Victoria because they went on to do a much better deal with Gillette!

Chapter 19

The following week Neil sent over the head of HR, Jeff Tepperman, to interview me and to review the conference that had taken place the previous week. The upshot of this was that I was suspended pending further enquiries.

It was the day before we were due to fly to Italy for the Palio. Neil was already in Italy and at the last minute he called Paul and told him to cancel the event. Paul spoke to me and I told him to tell Neil it was too late as the customers could not be contacted. I had already been banned from going but because it was via Simone's connection to the Piccolomini estate that the trip was made possible in the first place, she was leading the group.

The next morning I took Simone to the airport and left her with Richard to travel to Florence. That night Simone called me and said that over dinner Neil had been saying awful things about me and that she was very upset.

Incensed, I decided to ignore the ban and travel to Italy the next day. By this stage most of my credit cards were maxed out but I still had my original airline ticket and there was a hire car reservation in my name.

I went to Gatwick for an afternoon flight and when I got to the desk I was told that my ticket had been cancelled. I explained that I had to get to Florence and bought a new ticket for a flight in the evening. I just about had enough money on one card to pay for it but it was touch and go.

When I got to Florence around ten pm the hire car office was still open and they had my reservation. It had not been cancelled and was pre-paid. Phew!

I drove to Siena and hooked up with Simone and talked for a couple of hours about what Neil had been saying. By this time we were drawn together again. I was not in a depressed state and more like the person that she knew at the start of our relationship.

The next morning was the day of the Palio and a minibus picked our group up and went on to pick up a second group that were staying in a different location. Neil and Sandy were part of this group and his mouth dropped when he saw me. He sensibly did not make a scene and just went with the flow. When we got to Siena we were dropped at the top of the city and made our way to the centre for a light lunch. We then settled into our seats for what is the most amazing spectacle imaginable.

The following poem from Hole in my Soul is my description of the events that followed:

Palio

Dawn creeps up and lights the majesty of Il Campo, there is an eerie still before the storm of the Palio

A magnificent theatre with tawny facades, the perfect setting for this game of charades

This race of pride is now ten centuries old, the winning rider, brave and bold

There are no saddles to keep them in the seat, getting round and staying on a marvellous feat

The seventeen districts vying for first place, emotions' running high, this is not just a race

Spectators flock and fill this natural stadium, waiting as if for gladiators in their coliseum

The masses congregate in the centre ring, an elegant few at restaurants in tired seating

As the day progresses and the tension mounts, the riders know that it is only winning that counts

The horses are taken to the chapel and blessed, the shirts of the riders bearing their districts crest

At the starting rope the riders jockey for position, false starts delay for some their lifelong ambition

Finally they are off and race for the first turn, the excitement now raging as their muscles burn

Positions change as there are few rules, crashing and bumping, driving their mules

It's over too quick and the winner is enthroned, The King of Siena, for that day at least, the title is loaned

And after the finish the crowds flood on to the track, fighting breaks out, tears can't be held back

For all but the winner a gloom has descended, spirits forlorn and lives upended

As dusk settles down and the fervour quells, tables and chairs and all round cooking smells

The day leaves an imprint deep in your soul, a timeless wonder, you feel more whole.

After the race we had dinner in the restaurant and during the fabulous meal the Contessa Piccolomini paid us a visit. Simone and I had already met her on our earlier visit and chatted and thanked her for laying on such a brilliant day. Neil and Sandy came over and were like two kids begging for buttermilk!

We left Siena late that night and travelled back to the Piccolomini Estate. The following morning we had a meeting with Argos in one of the villas. Neil and Sandy came over and Neil asked to speak to me in private.

He asked me what I was doing there because he had expressly told me not to come. I told him that he left me no choice because of what he had told Simone. He was embarrassed and tried to brush it off but by then I was on a roll. I knew that the people in the meeting could hear us and I reminded him of the fact that he had been trying to get me to fire Paul for several months. He decided to leave and I was so angry I nearly through him down the stairs.

Later in the day I got a message that I was to get back to London straight away and for me to meet with Neil at his hotel. I told the messenger that if that was what was wanted they could send a private jet to pick me up!

Simone and I did not return for a couple of days. I knew I was going to be fired so what the hell.

I was fired.

Simon Russell

Chapter 20

Remington paid me about £30,000 in lieu of notice so it was tax free. I was also owed about ten grand in expenses but in turn owed Simone a similar amount. I deposited the 30k in an account I opened with the Halifax to protect the money from my creditors. I also paid Simone the money I owed her.

During July and I August I tried to get some things going under my own name.

I had met an Icelandic man called Einar Einarsson who had invented and patented a new form of eye ware. He had spent over £300,000 on tooling and development in the UK and as promotional item his cost in the UK was too high. I connected him to a sourcing agent friend of mine in Hong Kong, Henry Feng, and his unit cost was cut by 60% to 70%. He could have also got it tooled for nothing. I suspected that he had been ripped off royally by the people he had been working with over here.

I made connections for Einar all over the place and tried my best to promote and develop the business for him. I made contact with Pepsi and Coke and even put on a launch event at a restaurant in Brockenhurst followed by an open air concert featuring Mark Knopfler at Beaulieu House. I tried every which way I could to get the product off the ground but it just would not fly. It cost me dear too financially.

I did manage to successfully get 'We Will Rock You' to sponsor an all-girl crew for Cowes week. Roger Taylor came down to Southampton to personally launch the project. Hannah White the skipper was thrilled. Sadly it didn't earn me any money but I did get a lot of satisfaction in pulling it off.

I also tried to promote some local artists but that was like pushing water uphill!

Simone by this stage was working part time as a bar maid in the Lickfold Inn near Midhurst. This gave me some 'me' time down in my beloved New Forest – my final resting place I hope! She did get suspicious and one night when I was down there she called me and told me that I had been seen taking some girls back into a hotel. It was completely untrue but it told me that she had a spy in the camp. I also thought I knew who it was.

The next time we down there together we went to Fat Cats and I took the gun in the inside of my jacket pocket. I spoke to the manager of the bar, a South African girl, and opened up my jacket for her to see the gun. She went ballistic and screamed the place down. The bar was cleared and the police were called. Simone and I immediately left and went into the Stanford House Hotel just round the corner.

I ditched the gun in a large potted plant and when the police came and searched me they obviously did not find anything. In fact they were very apologetic and said that they thought it must have been a false alarm. Things like that did not happen in sleepy Lymington.

Needless to say things could have worked out very differently. Later that night I grabbed Simone's mobile phone, the source of so much shit, and threw it in the harbour!

Come the end of August I knew I was fucked. I had not managed to get anything going down there and it was time to leave.

I informed the agent that I was vacating the flat and one Sunday Simone and I drove down in a van and collected all my furniture and belongings.

I loved Lymington and have always enjoyed being close to the sea. It was very sad day as we drove up the high street and I left for the last time!

Chapter 21

In fairness to Simone and after all we had been through she could have left me down in Lymington to fry in my own juices. She must have felt that we still had a future together because she was prepared to re-integrate me back into her family environment.

My own situation was dire. By then I had about £20,000 in the bank but had debts that had mounted to in excess of £130,000. The only debt that was secured was on the car and that soon went when I stopped making the payments.

Barclays was major creditor. They rather stupidly had allowed me to excessively exceed my overdraft limits and across the two accounts and credit cards with combined limits of about £35,000 they had allowed me to rack up a debt in excess of £70,000. The remainder of the debt was spread across four or five credit cards, the loan on the car which would not be paid off by the sales price at auction and some personal debt of close to £10,000 owed to Beaulieu Events and a restaurant in Brockenhurst.

I was well and truly in a hole. I knew that getting another job in the same line of work, having been sacked and unwell twice, was virtually impossible. The only option open to me was to get some local work to put bread on the table and to try and ply myself as marketing consultant.

The local job came in the form of an assistant in a deli and café in Midhurst. I could walk to it, work from eight to four and then go home and work on the consultancy options. Working in the deli was obviously a big come down and I spent most of the time hiding in the back making sandwiches. It was owned by a lovely lady called Alison and she could feel my pain. In fairness she also paid me above the going rate – I think that I got £6 per hour!

Whilst doing this I continued to try and help Einar with his eye ware product but we kept ending up down more and more blind alleys.

My mental health was once again poor. I had become depressed again. I had seen my life fall dramatically apart once again, and Einar and Simone apart, all the people that I had helped evaporated.

I went back to see Dr Sherrington who had a clinic in Midhurst. She again diagnosed me with depression and put me back on anti-depressants. She would see me regularly and gave me a care coordinator who saw me weekly. I was still not seeing the boys and this furthered deepened my depression. They had made it clear that they did not want to see me all the time I was with Simone.

For a few months a relative peace descended. I played the role of step dad as best as I was able. I staved off the creditors and simply told them that I did not have any money to pay them. I saw the Citizens Advice Bureau and they wrote to all my creditors to explain the situation and that once I was back in my normal type of employment I could consider entering into a voluntary arrangement with them.

Simone remained positive and supportive. She knew I was ill again and did her best to be understanding. She was still working in the Lickfold and with her small income from there, her tax credits, Rob's contribution and my paltry £200 per week we able to get by.

Just after Christmas 2003 Simone came into the Deli one morning and shut us in the kitchen. She told me that my sixteen year old niece, Becky, had died!

I immediately drove Simone's car over to Lingfield to see my sister. I had never seen and will never forget the grief on Jenny's face. Becky had woken up the previous morning and said they she did not feel well. By the evening, and despite valiant attempts to save her, she had died. We were all in shock and worried about Jenny who was inconsolable.

I left later that evening and my mother stayed with Jenny that night and through the terrible process of visiting the hospital and undertaker to see the body.

Simone and I went to the funeral together. Kim and boys did not.

Death of a child

Where ever you are we know it's not far
Your love abounds, beautiful sounds
Mum is in pain, sees no gain
An incredible loss, we all give a toss
Priests and Kings, have more important things
Disease can be cured, if money is lured
We will do our best, to prevent the rest
Following your fate, before it's too late

Not too long, we'll sing the same song
Where ever you are, we know it's not far.

Heavily impacted by Becky's death I decided in the early spring of 2003 to use some of my residual money to get a place of my own. I wanted to see my own children. Because of my lack off creditworthiness I put down six months deposit on a small two bedroom house in Pulborough, about five miles from where the boys were living in Storrington. I also bought an old Audi for about £3000.

Simone was very unhappy but I think could see the merits of the plan. I also quit my job at the Deli and during the days went to the house in Pulborough and used it is an office to try and drum up some full time work or some sort of consultancy arrangement. I had not given up on Einar and continued to try and find customers for his product now we had got the sourcing and pricing rectified.

Einar was a good pal. He understood mental illness because his wife Linda had suffered badly. He had trained originally to be a priest and had a wonderful way about him, slightly mad and eccentric but a good friend to have.

By early summer I had still not drummed up any work and my money was running out. Having never been workshy I saw an advertisement for taxi drivers in Chichester. I duly applied, sorted out the paperwork and references and started work in June.

I had the early morning shift and had to leave the house at 5.30am for a 6.0am start in the centre of Chichester. My first big job every day was to pick up three severely disabled children and to take them to a day centre half an hour away in Worthing. A truly humbling experience!

I did the taxi job through the summer and supplemented it with bar work.

My wonderful grandmother who lived in Bournemouth died around this time. As a child I spent every summer holiday with her and my granddad at their beach hut in Boscombe. She was a truly special Nana and I miss her desperately.

By the end of the summer I was still not seeing the boys and finally decided to sever the knot with Simone. Once and for all this time!

Einar had already said that he could help me either within my relationship with Simone or if I choose to break up with her he would support me through that separation. In the end I decided I would go for separation, as hard as that was going to be. I felt it was the only way to be sure I got access to the boys and felt it would also help with the horrendous depression I was suffering again.

In early September I finally wrote her a letter and posted it through her letter box. I knew that I could not do it face to face. Strange as it may sound I still really loved her. Our relationship had truly been fire and ice and we were, at times like two sticks of dynamite but I did love her and very, very deeply.

That weekend I camped out at Einar's and ignored the phone calls from Simone. He helped me make the house in Pulborough more homely. I had not been staying there at nights since I had moved in, choosing instead to sleep with Simone.

By this time I managed to drum a small amount of consultancy work with a very nice guy called Robin Baker. He had a small consumer products based in Kensington that sold products to Boots and Superdrug. Robin had started life as a ballet dancer and by his own admission was not the greatest business man.

I quit my job at both the pub and the taxi company so I could concentrate on my work with Robin that I also thought might lead to other things.

In an effort to try and get Simone out of my system I went to see my brother- in-law, Martyn, who with my sister Sue owned a farm house in South West France. Martyn and I had always got on well. Sue at the time was still teaching in a school in Croydon. I stayed with Martyn for about ten days and by the end of the trip I felt that, with his help, I had got Simone out of my system. I hadn't!

On my return I bumped into an old friend, Sammy, who had split up from her husband John. John and I had seen quite a lot of each other over the last year or so and had too been helpful in my separation from Simone. That night Sammy and I met at my house in Pulborough and had sex. She was a smashing girl, a real earth mother and the two of us regularly had sex and really enjoyed each other's company.

At the time I was still seeing John, who was in love with Sammy despite their separation. It was important to keep Sammy and my relationship confidential therefore.

Around the same time I got a call from Simone one night asking me if I fancied a fuck. I could not help myself and went over to her house and we made love for the last time. I did continue to see her for some time and until I got an email from her one night telling me that she had found someone new.

I was devastated. Even though I had Sammy, who I was very fond of, I always hoped that Simone and I would get back together at some point. Maybe we still will!

I had already started going high again and was spending nights in cheap hotels in London.

The next phase of my heady journey was about to kick off and kick off in a big way!

Simon Russell

Chapter 22

I was dangerously high again. I was smoking weed and had used cocaine on one occasion in Chelsea. The ride was just about to get a whole lot scarier!

Psychospace

As I enter the world of psychospace, my brain and body no longer in place
The final kick that hurls me out, happens so fast, no time to shout
When I first arrive it's an amazing feeling, freedom, fulfilment and sexual healing
King of the World, Master of the Universe, solutions for everything, however perverse
No time for sleep, there are people to meet, got to spread the word, tell of my feat
The answers are there to everyone's prayers, sent to earth down the ethereal stairs
Tearing around fuelled by adrenaline and dope, preaching to the unwary, delivering false hope
As the hours pass and the story is told, worry sets in, paranoia takes hold
In this place there is no illusion, my mind is not deranged, there is no confusion
The power fades, the reality dawns, my space is invaded by the devil's pawns
Psychospace is a place where I feel, happy and strong and up in heel,
Everyone says 'you must not go again', one of these trips you are bound to be slain
But it's ok for them, they have not been, to Heaven and Hell and seen what I have seen.

One night I was in the Portobello Gold and asked a group if they would look after my bag while I went to the toilet. I was scheduled to go back to Pulborough that evening but things worked out differently. When I got back to the group one of them asked me if I would buy him an Absinthe for looking after my bag. I bought the whole group including myself an Absinthe.

We got on well and went to a nightclub. In the end I was left with a gorgeous girl called Asha Kirkby who as a result of being an in-line skating teacher was as fit as a fiddle. We ended up back in a flat that she was borrowing in the East End of London. Asha was a Buddhist and after much chanting and weed smoking we finally end up of having sex. I remember it well because as we came I could hear cheers from the flat next door. It was not us they were cheering – it was the English success in the final of the Rugby World Cup down under.

At about the same time and in the Portobello Gold again I met Rob Lowe. He had just done a round the world trip that took in the rugby final in Australia. I was chatting at the bar with Rachel Ward who was a political journalist at GMTV. Rachel wanted to interview Rob who was being very loud and pretty obnoxious.

We went up to his room and chatted with him for a while. He was an IT expert who had worked on the 3G program and was currently working as a consultant at HMRC in Southend. We had a fun night and left Rob in the early hours. Rachel and I slept together without having sex and after breakfast the next morning she headed off.

Rob came down from his room and we went for a walk down the Portobello Road. At one point he stopped and walked on his hands for twenty metres or so. A little further on he stopped again and asked me if I thought he could strip off naked, run over to one of the clothes stalls and get dressed again in under a minute. He did it, to much applause and laughter from the spectators.

Rob was wild and I think a manic depressive too. This was the start of a short but highly destructive relationship that would see me sectioned for the first time.

That weekend I met Asha on the beach front at Brighton. After a good lunch Asha made her excuses and left. I walked along the beach and found a bar to drink in and lounge around thinking about Asha. Later I got chatting with a small group of people that included a beautiful black girl. Her name was Yolande Bath and she was very upfront in telling me that she was recovering from a cocaine addiction, had been thrown out by her husband and was living in a hostel and was bi-sexual. I took Yolande home with me that night feeling very good about myself.

Around about the same time I had decided to move house again. Buoyed up by my work with Robin and in a very high state I had signed up for a farmhouse in the village of Iping near Midhurst. It was a beautiful wooden house called Manor Farm House, right by the fast flowing River Rother. It had three good sized bedrooms a large kitchen diner and a sitting room with wonderful views over the open countryside.

I told Yolande that she could move in with me. The two of us moved in together in the middle of December. We had separate rooms and she paid rent. I was still seeing Sammy at the time and also still nursed the desire to get back with Simone who I was back in touch with.

One night I took Yolande round to Sammy's flat in Pulborough. As I sat down Sammy came over and undid my trousers and started riding me. I looked over at Yolande and she simply smiled and started to get undressed. We had an amazing threesome and Sammy fulfilled one of her ambitions to have sex with another woman. An ambition in my experience held by many women.

Rob and I charged around the country with each other in his Jaguar. I went up to his home town of Duffield in Derbyshire where he lived in a converted castle. I met his wife but she did not want to meet me. She did not want to see Rob either. She thought he was ill.

I was so deluded I thought I was working for him as his number two and he would pay me £800 per day. I neglected Robin. We were on a big bender. One morning in Duffield I got my hair cut off and created havoc amongst the shopkeepers.

Rob also came to Iping and one night we paid a visit to Sarah Miles, the two times Oscar winning British actress who lived in a beautiful house in the neighbouring village of Chithurst. Sarah was regarded as a little eccentric – apparently she drank her own urine and had buried her ex-husband, Robert Bolt, in the garden.

Sarah claimed to have been cured from cancer many years previously, in the 60's I think, and still had the glass equipment that had been used to effect the cure. Rob and I spent a little time with Sarah over a couple of days. We walked her dogs with her and had our pictures taken with her and her two Oscars.

I became convinced in my psychotic state that Sarah was in fact my mother and gave her a book of plants with a little passport picture of each of my sons inside. I thought that my father was one of the great directors, designers or musicians of the time, who she would have obviously been in touch with. Various names came to mind, Fellini, Versace and Zeffirelli were just a few of the potential candidates. I knew he was Italian because I felt sure I had Italian blood.

I was stark raving bonkers!

One night in Iping, when Rob told me I was not going to be paid, I locked myself in the sitting room with his briefcase and phone, and a large hunting knife that I had bought. I threatened to destroy his sim card and rip the contents of his briefcase to threads unless he paid me the money he owed me. I was violent and very threatening.

Rob managed to calm me down and set off the next day. That would be the last I saw of him.

That same day Yolande told me that she had not managed to beat her Cocaine addiction and I went mad with her. I told her that I wanted my children back and there would be no way of doing that if I had an addict living under the same roof. I brandished the same hunting knife at her and left the house. When I got back she was gone and like Rob I would never see her again. Who could blame her!

I met Simone one night around the same time at the Angel Hotel in Midhurst. It was a very tense meeting. I still loved her. I still wanted her. I was very ill and I am sure she knew. I told her about Sammy and she went completely mental. She went outside into the street and ran her keys down the side of my car and threw a gift I had bought her into the street. That was the last time I saw Simone!

That was the last I would see of my car for a few days too. Yolande had got together with Rob and because I had taken a £500 deposit from her for the purchase of the car it was taken by a Southend based guy called Del Boy! I still had the log book though.

I was due to go to my sisters on Christmas day but instead spent it with Sammy.

In my psychotic state I went off in her car to where Sarah Payne had been killed and thinking I was an investigator extraordinaire searched rubbish sacks at the end of the lane. I found prescription drug packets and later took them to the police station in Midhurst. I told the police that I had unearthed a paedophile ring and named various local people that I believed to be part of it.

That night I checked into the Spread Eagle Hotel in Midhurst and joined the Christmas party goers. Rob had given them a credit card to confirm my reservation.

Later in the evening I was called to reception to say the credit card had been rejected and I was asked to leave. I tried to protest but the hotel manager was insistent. They escorted me back to my room to clear it out and once there I said I was not leaving.

A short time later the police came and they asked the manager to try and escort me off the premises. As he approached I pretended that he slapped me across the face, the police rushed over and pepper gassed and handcuffed me. I then spent the night in the cells in Chichester. I screamed and shouted the house down all night and eventually they drove me back to Midhurst the following morning without charge.

On Boxing Day it turned out That Rob too had spent Christmas day in the cells. He told me that he had been caught with a toy gun and the police arrested him.

He got a mutual friend and business contact, Peter Clarke, to take me to the Goodwood Park Hotel and to pay for my room and leave his card details for me to charge against.

That evening I went to the resident's dinner and sat at a table with a group of strangers. At one point I went to the toilet and the next thing I knew I was laying on the car park floor surrounded by paramedics. I had been attacked as I left the toilet and could feel pain in my face and my leg.

The paramedics asked me if I wanted to go to hospital but I just asked them to get me back to my room. I must have fallen in to a deep sleep and woke up nursing a shiner and a limp. I called down to reception and asked them what had happened. They told me that I had been attacked by a group of gypsies that were staying in the hotel. Apparently they took a disliking to me and punched and kicked me and dumped me in the car park. The police had not done anything about it because they were worried about inflaming the situation.

The hotel were very apologetic but suggested that I leave straight away. I was incensed and noticed that the TV was in a position whereby it could, attached to the mains, reach the bath. I phoned reception and told them I was suicidal and they had illegally placed the TV in such a way as it could help me achieve my goal. I filled the bath and dumped the TV in it.

The head of security came to the room and escorted me off the property.

I didn't have a penny in my pocket and decided to limp slowly the four or five miles to Chichester. I tried calling Peter Clarke but he did not want to know. Apparently I had charged a brand new golf driver, which I was using as a walking stick and some new clothes to his credit card.

When I got to Chichester I called my parents and they organised a cab to take me up to their house in Purley. I arrived in the early evening and spent the night in their sitting room with my dad's air rifle in my lap. I was convinced the establishment was after me. I wasn't sure who I was but I was clearly someone they wanted to terminate. I also became convinced that my dad, who was not really my dad, was part of the security services charged with protecting my mum and me.

I even became convinced that my mum was the rightful heir to the throne!

I looked through some fashion magazines as I stayed on guard all night. Every model in the magazine was Simone or that was how it looked to me.

The next day Del Boy came to my parents. We had a cooked breakfast and he took me back to Iping. En route we stopped by at Sammy's and she and I had quick shag on a kitchen counter.

Chapter 23

Del Boy took me to Iping, dropped me off and said he would be back in due course. It was now the 28th of December and paranoia had set in a major way. Sammy came over one day but could see I was ill and left. That was the last I would see of her too.

On New Year's Eve I got talking on the internet to Julie Pigott, an artist based in Northampton. I told her that I was the son of Sarah Miles and Gianni Versace and the establishment wanted to kill me. I needed somewhere safe to hole up for a while. She agreed and said that I could come to her the following morning.

Sammy's husband John owed me £300 and he reluctantly agreed to meet me the following morning in Storrington and he would have the £300. He said he might also have a glass that he would smash in my face. The next morning I had a taxi pick me with my luggage that included the golf club and hunting knife for protection. I got out of the car with the golf club and offered it to John as a present. He gave me the money and told me to fuck off. That was the last that I saw of John.

The taxi took me to Chichester and dropped me off the taxi office. This was the same one that I had worked for the previous summer. I needed to do some shopping and asked in the office if they would look after my bags which included the golf club and the knife.

When I returned from shopping the police were there and they took me for my second trip to the police station in Chichester.

I was held in the waiting area where the duty sergeant sits high up behind a big operations desk. I had to empty all my pockets and all my belongings got bagged up and I signed for them. I was taken to a cell and outside had to take off my shoes and belt and put them in a locker.

I was told that I would be held there until a mental health team could be assembled to review my mental state and capacity. The cell was about five metres square and had a metal toilet in one corner and a mattress on a plinth under the window.

The police were very kind and helpful. They brought me food and hot drinks and allowed me out into a courtyard every now and again for a smoke. By this stage I had sharply come down off my high and felt certain I could pass the interview with the panel that were to determine my mental health position.

The following morning I was taken from the cell and into a meeting room to be greeted by Dr Sherington and two other people. One I think was a social worker and the other a lay person or judge.

They asked me all sorts of questions about who I was, who my parents were and what I did for a living. I answered them all in a factually correct and polite and calm way. I can be very plausible in situations like this. However, they were aware of the knife, the golf club, the assault at the Goodwood Park Hotel and the incident at the Spread Eagle Hotel in Midhurst.

I think they also spoke to my mum and dad who would have told them what I was like with the gun on the day after Boxing Day. I was sectioned and much to my anger and disgust I taken to the Centurion Mental Health Unit at St Richards hospital Chichester.

I was pissed off in the extreme. I had been on my way to Northampton to see Jules. The establishment had got me! Worse still my parents had joined forces with the establishment. Once I had gone through the ritual of having my clothes and belongings identified and entered on to a sheet of paper to sign and been shown to my room I called my dad.

The only person able to get you off a section immediately is your next of kin and in doing so they have to declare that they will take care of you. I told him that there had been a terrible mistake and I needed his help. He replied that he could not help me and that I was to take the medication and do what I was told!

I knew that I was in the shit. It was a locked ward and worse still I was to be interviewed by a forensic psychiatrist to see if I merited an even higher security ward. I managed to pass that test and they must have concluded that I was not a danger to myself or others on that ward.

Soon after being admitted and probably due to the stress of being locked up I thought that I was someone special again and that I was here for my own protection from those who wanted me killed. The doors were locked to prevent anyone getting in and not to stop me going out.

The staffing was like the United Nations and many were from the African continent. In my deluded state I believed that they knew I was the new leader of the free world. All the staff wore casual clothes and were very pleasant and respectful

That first night I refused to take any medication and it was not forced down me. The nurses that came to give it to me when I was in bed decided that I was OK and unless you are being aggressive or unruly you do have the right to refuse medication.

The one thing I noticed about the other patients was how intelligent they were. I don't know what I expected but I was surprised.

The set up was pretty simple. There was a mixed bedroom wing all with single en-suite rooms. A large lounge. A nurse's station and office. There was a kitchen and eating area and a games area with a table tennis table. There was also a dispensary.

Imagine the night

The sign says hospital but you are really not sure, unaware of an illness, no need for a cure

The doors are locked but you can see inside, anxiety building like an incoming tide
The door is released, you are welcomed in, no uniform in sight, not sure of your sin
Escorted to a room, another locked door, ragged and bedraggled, possessions on the floor
The black sack is emptied, an inventory taken, increasingly nervous, frightened and shaken
With all weapons of minor destruction removed, you begin your internment until sanity is proved
Long corridors stretch from the admin hub, a TV room with a patient battling a stub
School like dining room, quiet between meals, the soft furnished lounge where the spirit congeals
Off to your room, whitewashed and stark, signs of former patients have made their mark

A radiator belts out interminable heat, a plastic layer under the single bed sheet
Wash basin and mirror unbreakable of course, the window designed to resist the greatest force
An OT area to paint pointless pictures, doctor's offices for your weekly fixtures
Most important of all, it is why you are here, the cocktail bar that dispenses its cheer
Peace is broken with screams and cries, alarms are sounded, nurses rush like flies
This is not a place you would want to visit, it corrodes your senses, and things just don't fit
You want to turn away, take rapid flight, it's bad during the day, just imagine the night.

I think that it was this early on that I decided that I was the love child of John F Kennedy and Marilyn Munroe. The staff members were there to protect me until my DNA would prove this to be correct. Nothing would shift me from this and I used to march around all day acting like the President. There was a garden with high fencing with a gate in it and a field behind. When the moment was right a helicopter would land and pick me up.

One morning I had to go to the main hospital for a blood test and an enormous African guy escorted me. I thought that he was my bodyguard.

The morning of my first doctors revue meeting came. I had made it clear that I did not want my parents there. My parents had died many years ago in America! I went into the meeting and my mother and sister were there smiling at me. They had driven for two hours to be there. I flew into a rage and demanded that they leave.

A little while later I relented and sat with them in the lounge. My mum, God love her, had brought a family tree to try and get me to understand that my dad and she were my parents and that Jenny was my sister. I showed them pictures of Simone and poems I had written and paintings I had painted. It was plainly clear that I was very unwell and they had been told that the psychosis may not be curable! I was very sad when they left.

Through the use and my acceptance of some powerful anti-psychotic medication such as Olanzapine and

Haloperidol I was gradually brought down to earth and within about four weeks I was allowed ground leave.

At some point during my stay as an inpatient Del Boy came down with the rest of the cash for the car. I think he gave me less than £1000 so together with the £500 I had got from Yolande I netted about half the value.

I had a couple of other visitors while I was there. Colin Dobson, who runs M4 design in Newbury and my very old friend John Bell both, plucked up the courage to come and have lunch with me. Surprisingly Kim also called to say how sorry that she was that I was there.

Whilst in hospital I also became friends with Victoria Hartman who I called Posh. There was also a GP called Alex Muir whose wife had left him to set up home with another woman. Alex broke out one night by smashing a window with a chair and made a break for freedom. He was quickly picked up by the police and returned to the unit.

After about four weeks I was allowed ground leave and could go over to the shop in the main hospital. Although I was not allowed I also went into Chichester which was about a twenty minute walk. There was a café in the grounds that sold cigarettes. Everyone smokes in mental hospitals!

A few weeks later I was told that I could go home and be seen by the home treatment team. I had come off the mega-high and the depression that follows like night after day had started to take a grip.

The letting agent asked me if I could leave as soon as possible and whatever happened I would not be able to stay beyond the six month contract date that expired in June. Without a car Iping is a nightmare. I had little or no money. The oil tank had run out and the place was freezing.

One night Jules drove all the way from Northampton with an electric radiator to help keep me warm.

By April I was in a desperate state and my parents came to see me. They agreed that I could move back in with them in Purley until I got my life back on track. That was to take some time!

Simon Russell

Chapter 24

My parents were in their seventies at the time and it was very generous hearted of them to take me in. I had been diagnosed by Dr Sherrington as having manic depression (bi-polar affective disorder) which is a chronic and incurable condition.

My mum had been a nurse all her life and had a naturally caring nature. My dad could see the practical issues I faced and they came together to help me as much as they could.

Soon after moving in I got terrible pains in my gut. I went to the GP and was sent for a variety of tests which all proved inconclusive. Still in great pain I took myself off to A and E one night and demanded some attention and action.

I was admitted into Mayday Hospital in late 2004 and after some tests that involved the nuclear medicine department at the Royal Marsden it was concluded that I had a bowel stricture that needed to be removed.

I had the surgery and was in excruciating afterwards. I had a morphine pump that only dispenses every half hour or so but it did help overcome the unbelievable pain. I found the standard of care in Mayday at the time simply appalling. The staff used to bitch and argue with each other. Patient's needs were not met – I even used to witness a person a few beds down from me who could not feed himself have his food tray taken away without him having touched a drop.

One person in particular sticks in mind from that first experience at Mayday. Ray Hoffman. He came in for a routine procedure and left in a box. It seemed to me and his wife Joy that he would have been better off not going near the place. A real tragedy!

I was lucky in that my Mum came in every day and brought me some good nutritious food. She also spotted things that were wrong like empty drips and morphine pumps and rallied some help to get replacements.

Shortly after the first operation I met a wonderful lady, Fiona Mackley, on the internet. Her husband had left her with the three young children and to bring them up in the best way possible she had become a child minder.

After a month or two chatting on line she invited me over one night to erect some bunk beds in her son's room. DIY is not my speciality but I did make a success, with her help, of that little task. We soon became friends and lovers.

I was applying for jobs again at the time and had some interest from a company called Rexel up in Aylesbury. They were in the office supplies business and were looking for someone in their international business.

I was still feeling the after effects of the surgery and was still in the depressed phase of my manic depression but my mother got me up at seven every day to work away on my applications.

I went for an assessment day in in London for the Rexel job and took a bottle of Oramorph to help me get through the day. I met with the US president and thank God he did not think I was a good fit.

Shortly afterwards the same pain returned and I was again admitted to Mayday. This time the doctors knew the cause and after a few checks confirmed that yet again I had a bowel stricture probably caused by Chrohns disease. I had another very painful operation and this time I was fortunate in that I had both my mum and Fiona to look after me whilst I was in Stalag Mayday.

This time an ex-postman with dodgy legs was in the bed next to me. One night after screaming in pain he tried to get out of bed but fell. Within a week he was dead. I offered to co-operate with his niece who was stunned when she heard that he died. I could see from my bed the hospital staff close ranks!

After several months of rest and recuperation I was back at the computer looking for work again. Towards the end of 2005 I spotted an advertisement for a commercial manager to help run a small conglomerate of little businesses that included a chain of eight or so pharmacies, a garden centre and a conference venue in Kingston. It was paying 60k and it seemed like the perfect re-entry for me if I could get through the interview process unscathed.

Chapter 25

Doctor Philip Brown. That is a name I will take to my grave for a raft of reasons. Entirely unpleasant ones that make me question our society and those at the top of it.

Doctor Philip Brown – now he is a case.

For many years he very successfully owned and ran a publishing business called PJB Publishing. The principle magazine was called Scrip. It was a journal for the Pharmaceutical industry. In the years before he sold the business in 2005 it had a turnover in the region of £20million and a pre-tax profit of circa £10million. A great business and nothing wrong with that.

He sold the business for in excess of £150 million to the Informa Group. Great sales price and nothing wrong with that either.

Instead of retiring on the proceeds of the sale and possibly doing something philanthropic his sole pre-occupation to me seemed to be the recovery of as much of the tax he had paid through something called roll over relief. Roll over relief entitles you to recover tax paid if you invest in new businesses.

Phillip in his wisdom bought a Conference Centre called Warren House and a Garden Centre called Pantiles. He also bought a group of individual pharmacies and being a pharmacist this was at least close to his knowledge, skills and understanding.

My job as commercial manager was to intervene where required to bring commercial expertise and develop strategies. Most of the pharmacies were making money but they all had a list of things that needed doing. The garden centre was a basket case and the conference centre, whilst an amazing property, was struggling financially.

I was still struggling physically and mentally. Because of my ability to elevate my mood when tired and exhausted I was able to rise to the challenge ahead.

The first week, which was at the end of January 2006, I spent in the office in Richmond, reading up on all the acquisitions and meeting Ian, Phillip's PA, Peter his brother and Sanjay the accountant. I did not hear from or see Phillip at all that week.

The following few weeks I concentrated on the pharmacies and visited them all. They were all in East Sussex and Kent. As part of my package I was given a hire car to race around the different locations.

Over the course of the next four or five weeks I developed a strategy for the business which in essence had a list of things to do per branch, the development in all branches of their care home business, the introduction of home delivery in all branches, a greater focus on pharmacy services and less on the personal care and beauty products. Finally I wanted to cap the strategy off with a new name and identity that all branches would trade under. I even looked into names like Pharmacy First. Philip didn't like this and told me in no uncertain terms that he was the boss and he made the decisions. I knew then that I was dealing with, in my opinion, a very unpleasant man.

One morning when I was driving down to Kent I somehow managed to drive my car into the back of a lorry and more or less write it off. Ian was very concerned and thought I should go home. Instead I rented a car from a rental chain and carried on with my day. The first car he had got from a taxi company that he used and there was a £500 excess on it.

The next time I saw Philip I told him that I had been involved in an accident. He said that he had heard and that it meant him losing his £500 excess. Not a word about how I might be. I ended up paying the excess and in the end I had to pay it to a lady I did not know at the request of the taxi company. All very dodgy! I now knew I was dealing with a very, very unpleasant man.

My next task was to sort out a warranty claim at the garden centre. There was a very nasty smell of sewerage every now and again and Phillip had to invest a substantial amount of money installing a large pumping system to take the sewage about one hundred metres to the main drainage system in the road outside.

My job was to find out what was causing the smell and to see if he could recover the cost of the work from the previous owners.

The first and most significant thing I discovered from the reports that I read was that the overflow from the septic tank went into a culvert that ran under the property and became a stream again in an adjoining property. The owner of the adjoining property had complained several times that his fish in his pond that was fed by the stream were dying.

In the sale contract the previous owners had lied and said that the overflow dissipated into the ground in a herringbone fashion. We had them lock stock and four smoking barrels.

The thing is that the reports I had been reading had been around for some time and I told Philip that he needed to be asking questions of his lawyer, surveyor and others who should have all picked up on this a long time before.

I compiled an enormous file with records of all the phone calls I had made and discussions had together with exhibits and photographs. I am not a lawyer but I am very proud of the job that I did to nail the previous owners.

The trouble was that I was going high again. I was not taking any drugs but I had started drinking heavily again.

I told Phillip that the information I wanted to present to him was potentially explosive – I think he thought I meant literally- but I meant as far as the consequences for his staff and advisors. I immediately became unpopular with all the idiots that he had surrounded himself with.

There were also some silly incidents with a crappy old lap top that I was accused of not putting back in the cupboard as I should have done. All rubbish and I suspected the work of his very jealous brother, Peter.

I got fired again.

Simon Russell

Chapter 26

It was early April 2006. I had seen the boys when Kim and brought them up to my parent's house shortly after I moved back two years earlier. By this time she had a new partner and I would see the boys from time to time.

The Saturday after I was fired I was due to pick Sam up from Storrington and take him to Jenny's house to celebrate my niece's, Vanessa's 21st birthday. I was dangerously high and stopped off at the Halifax to get a lump of cash. I had told Fiona that I was taking Sam away to Eastbourne after the party. I got waylaid in the bank because they wanted me to set up a deposit account for some of the severance money I had received from Philip. I think it was about £8,000 or £9,000 and they still owed me another £1500 or so in expenses.

I was horribly late for Sam and we consequently were very late for the party. It was a nervy time for Sam because he had not seen his cousins for about five years.

After the party I took Sam back to Storrington and after I left him I took myself off to Eastbourne.

At this time I again thought I was someone very special. Someone who went into dangerous situations and unearthed wrong doing. In this case I was convinced that I had discovered an IRA plot to poison London via this sewerage problem. I had to go into hiding. I was a Jason Bourne or James Bond figure.

Being one of those types of characters I had to act accordingly. I booked a suite in the Grand Hotel on Eastbourne seafront. I also booked a room at the Sherwood Hotel a few streets away so that I could move between the two in relative safety.

The first night I luxuriated in my suite at the Grand. It is a truly stunning hotel and it evokes wonderful times of the past. I went for a swim and a steam in the hotel spa got showered and went to the Carlisle Bar and Grill in Carlisle Road for dinner. It is no longer there but it was a fun place with great staff and good food.

I ordered a fillet of pork with a blue cheese sauce and crème brulee. I had to go into the kitchen and burn the top of the brulee myself because the chef had left when I was ready for it.

That night the staff and I bought some bottles and went back to the managers flat for a small party. Inevitably the weed came out and I ended up sleeping on the sofa. Pretty bizarre considering I actually I had two rooms to choose from within about one hundred metres either way.

The following morning I went out and got a full English takeaway from a great little Italian café on the corner of Carlisle Road and Compton Street. I took it back to the flat for the manager and me and then availed myself of her bath.

At lunchtime I went back to the Carlisle Grill to discuss arrangements for a party that I wanted to host there. They must have thought me really weird because I scoped out the whole place. I checked the back door and the back gate that led into a back passage wide enough for a car. I went through the place with a fine toothcomb looking for possible lapses in security. I asked them to get a quote to have all the glass converted to bullet proof. I told them that I worked with several very famous people as a security consultant - I was playing Kevin fucking Costner in the Bodyguard. I had completely lost it and they were open mouthed throughout.

That afternoon I went to my room at the Sherwood to mix things up a little and see if anyone was following me. I called Robert, who ran a high class escort service in the Sussex and Kent, and made a reservation with Laura for 11am on Monday in the lounge area in the atrium of the Grand. That night I got smashed in a local pub and listened to Elvis on the duke box all night. By the end of the evening I thought that he could also be my dad with Sarah Miles, Princess Margaret or Marilyn Munroe as my mother.

Monday morning I showered in my room at the grand and dressed in jeans and a nice shirt. I went downstairs at about 10.50am. I have always been a stickler for timekeeping especially where women are involved. I was excited. Robert had described a very beautiful and very bright girl to me. One who often got called to Washington D.C. to work.

I was not disappointed. At a few minutes to eleven Laura entered, smiled at me and asked if she could sit down. I was the only person there so there could be no confusion. She was dressed in a black pinstripe suit, white blouse and black stockings with high heels. She had shoulder length blonde hair, beautiful eyes and a smile to die for.

I ordered her some tea and we discussed my requirements. I was mesmerised. I said that it was a mixture of business and pleasure. I told her that I was a security consultant and that we needed to do a full sweep of the hotel looking for any issues. Then we would have some fun. I asked her if she would stay with me for twenty four hours. She was very happy with the arrangement and told me it would be £1500. I didn't quibble or look surprised and just said that would be fine and that we should go upstairs to arrange a bank transfer.

Once we upstairs I gave her my Halifax card and within minutes the transaction was complete and I could relax. I told her that I was going to have a swim and to make herself comfy until I got back. I ordered a bottle of champagne and told her to help herself when it arrived. I also left some cash for her to tip with.

When I got back she was standing on the balcony overlooking the sea with a glass of champagne in her hand. I joined her and toasted her. I told her how beautiful she was and what a joy this was going to be for me.

For the next hour or two we walked the hotel, went to places we shouldn't have, checked out the balconies at the front and the vulnerabilities. It was right out of the Bodyguard again. I don't know if she thought I was serious or not but she certainly enjoyed playing the game.

We then went off to a local pub and played pool and drank away the afternoon. She was very good and very nearly beat me a few times. When I am high all my senses are heightened and so playing darts or pool becomes much easier. We were in the same pub I had been in the night before and again had the duke box playing all afternoon.

Around six we went back to the Grand and hit the bar for cocktails. Laura had a great capacity for alcohol matched only by own. Laura insisted that we had Tanqueray 10 and tonic and loads of it. A little later I called the front desk and told them that we would eat in the room and could they also install a video and some cassettes.

At about eight we went up to the room and I ordered lobster for us both. I don't know why because I hate shellfish but it just seemed to be the right thing to do. The trolley was wheeled in and both in dressing gowns by this stage we sat for our meal. Laura devoured hers and most of mine and afterwards I went out onto the balcony and started talking to an imaginary crowd. I told them not to worry and that the world was safe in my hands.

I went back inside and knelt down in front of Laura who was on the sofa and parted her dressing gown. I kissed her neck and nipples and worked my way down to her vagina. I was there for ever breathing her wonderful smell and licking her clitoris as she rose and fell. We struggled to the bed and she rode me violently eventually coming in a fit of shudders. For some reason I couldn't come that night but it did not in any way spoil my enjoyment.

In the morning I found Laura sleeping on the floor. I asked why she was down there and apparently it was because I wouldn't shut up all night. I had no recollection of that.

Around ten am I said farewell to Laura. I don't know what she thought of the previous twenty three hours. She probably thought I was mad and she was right if she did.

Chapter 27

I turned on my mobile phone and there was a pile of missed calls and messages from Fiona. I called her back and explained that I had upset some pretty powerful people and was in hiding in Eastbourne. I told her I was safe and had a room at the Sherwood and one at the Grand. When it was safe I would be home. It would probably be in the next day or two.

Within about half an hour the police arrived at the Grand to question me. They took me to a private room and asked me what I had been up to. As far as I was concerned the police were just as much the enemy as the rest of the establishment. I told them that I had been fired from my job and was just having a rest in Eastbourne. Much to Fiona's chagrin I managed to blag them off and they left me alone. I was annoyed. Very very annoyed.

That night I stayed at the Sherwood because I did not want the police bothering me at the Grand again. I turned my phone off and had another good night in the pub. The next morning Fiona was on my trail again and she was mapping my moves around Eastbourne. Eventually I went back to the pub and was enjoying a game of pool when I was surrounded by police. There was no way out.

I was taken under protest to the Eastbourne detention centre where after taking blood they decided I was far too far over the limit to be questioned and they would leave me to sober up for six or seven hours.

Eventually I went in front of a sectioning panel who asked me all sorts of questions about my work and what I had been doing in Eastbourne. I managed to answer it all truthfully and without any embellishment. Apparently the panel phoned Fiona and checked what I said with her to which she said that it was all true. On that basis they said that they could not detain me. Fiona was persistent though and told them about the knife incident in Chichester and that was that – I was banged up for the night and sectioned. I was outraged and swearing blue murder.

The next day I was put in an ambulance with a police officer and taken to The Bethlem Royal Hospital. I thought I was being taken to a landing strip to board a private plane to a place of safety! God what a contrast. From The Grand

Hotel to a mental hospital within twenty four hours. Thank you Fiona.

The drill was much the same as at the Centurion. The staff was multi-national again. I thought that they were there to protect me from those trying to kill me. At one point when I was watching TV I thought we were in a Big Brother type situation and I pontificated to the screen in the same way as I had done on the balcony of the Grand Hotel a few days earlier.

I gave expansive speeches in the living area about how I had divided up the world and given Africa to Sam and the Americas to Joe to manage. I would be sailing round the world continuously, calling in on my protectorates to make sure the good guys were in charge.

There was an Asian lady called Mae. I held her hand one morning and apologised for the Vietnam War. After that she followed me everywhere and was eventually moved to another ward.

I was on the ground floor and I believed that Simone was upstairs. I tried every which way to get up there but to no avail.

The drug regime was the same – lots of anti-psychotics. Lots of stodgy food. Lots of weight gain.

My mum came to see me as often as she could and brought me fresh chicken sandwiches and lots of other goodies. She came on Sunday's and the two of us went to church.

As I started to come down from the high Fiona came and took me for an aids test. My mum and dad came and told me that I could not live with them when I was discharged. John Bell came and took me for lunch.

I was discharged around the end of June and moved into my own flat in Wallington. I felt terrible again – very low and suicidal.

Chapter 28

Reach Out

> *I want to reach out, I want to touch the sky*
> *The harder I try, the deeper the lie*
> *I want to reach out, to leave a vapour trail*
> *But my life is stale, destined to fail*
> *I want to reach out, don't want to be plain*
> *But the pain won't refrain, my soul has been slain*
> *I want to reach out, I want the thrill*
> *But they tell me I'm ill, just take the pill*
> *I want to reach out, at the speed of sound*
> *My spirit found, not flat on the ground*
> *I want to reach out, I want to hear the bird song*
> *Please tell me what's wrong, I am just drugged along*
> *I want to reach out, how hard I yell*
> *Can anyone tell, if I will go to hell.*

That Autumn I did reach out and I went to Phuket in Thailand.

I had read in a newspaper that prescription medicine could be purchased over the counter in Thailand and I decided because of my attraction to Buddhism and my love Asia that this would be a perfect place to die.

I really was feeling awful. I could not string a sentence together. I had lots of physical aches and pains. My bowels were very loose. I felt that the anti-psychotic medication slowed me down and fattened me up. I really did want to die.

I did not tell anyone of my plan. I simply told Fiona I was going to see an old friend, John Broom, for the day. Early one Monday morning I got a taxi to Heathrow and boarded a flight to Bangkok. I did not know how I was going to survive the flight. I felt so tired I thought I was going to pass out in the check in queue. I felt terrible about what I was doing to my boys, my parents and Fiona and her children. I just could not cope anymore with this overbearing depression.

When I arrived at Bangkok I called Fiona and told her where I was and why I was there. I had a connecting flight to Phuket to make and could not speak for long. She was shocked and surprised. I guess it is just not a normal thing for someone to do. But as she knew by then I was not a normal person.

Fiona had known almost from the outset of our relationship that I had bi-polar but she had not seen me in action until my trip to Eastbourne and the subsequent high and low. She did not run though and helped me through some very difficult times –even though I was not always appreciative because no-one on a high wants to come down.

Fiona also had a good relationship with my mum and they supported each other well. I had formed a strong relationship with her three children, Josh, Amber and Joe and had a special closeness to Joe who was about four when I first met him in 2005.

I flew onto Phuket and arrived at my resort hotel on the Tuesday afternoon. I called Fiona again and told her where I was staying.

I went to bed that afternoon and did not leave my room for twenty four hours. What a contrast to Eastbourne. I was in one of the party capitals of the world but I was racked with exhaustion. I had no interest in drinking or meeting women.

On the Wednesday night I went out in search of my pills and bought sixty Tramadol tablets and ten Zopiclone. That should do it! I went back to the hotel to formulate a plan.

I don't know exactly what stopped me. Fiona's gentle persuasion, the hurt it would cause to my loved ones or a lack of balls. I would like to think it was a combination of all three but the latter was definitely a key factor. I have often felt that you have to be completely beyond desperation to take your own life. It is so final and a bit of me always remained slightly optimistic.

I came back about three or four days earlier than planned and paid a supplement for the privilege.

I got back to Heathrow and a taxi took me home. As far as everyone was concerned it was as if I had not been away. That was everyone other than Fiona who told me that she could not have a relationship with someone who wanted to commit suicide. That was the end of our relationship.

2007 was the eye of the storm.

Chapter 29

Shortly after I returned from Thailand my landlord served me notice and I had two months to find a new flat. With my illness I am classified as a vulnerable adult and the council are duty bound to provide accommodation at all times.

Luckily a flat was immediately available in Carshalton and I went to view it straight away. The landlord, John Eggleton, was there and I liked him and I really liked the flat. It had everything I needed. It was ground floor flat, it had a good sized kitchen/diner come sitting area, a double bedroom and a power shower. I said that I would take it. It was a block of six on three floors and John, who lived in France, owned the two ground floor flats and the one above mine.

Carshalton was a much better location for me because it is a small village and everything was on hand. It was also the place of my birth in 1959.

Ring Road

I started and finished in exactly the same place, around the ring road at double the pace

Now back at the beginning with nowhere to go, the end of the road and the end of the show

No earlier memories before the crack to my head, the scar a talking point in the life I've led

But was the damage deeper than first thought, did it create the hole in which my life was caught

I had some successes along the way, reasons for joy at work and play

But continuity evaded me, difficult to sustain, the twists and turns only causing pain

The highest of highs the birth of my boys, watching them grow and playing with their toys

Determined not to be a part time dad, but alone now without them and terribly sad

All I wanted was a life by the sea, my wife, my children, my work and me

To hear the sound of gulls and waves, my family and me not consumer slaves

I experienced the rush of love in my veins, like a connection direct to the mains

But my illness took over and I had to let go, to preserve her own soul and let her life flow

There was a period of bliss in my mid to late twenties, when life seemed to pass with consummate ease

But it wasn't enough, I had a hunger for more, with my foot on the accelerator, I hit the floor

Going so fast I lost sight of the road, a breakdown inevitable, I could not be slowed

Blinded by bright lights and the rush for success, I ignored the warnings and drove to excess

I was sent for repairs and wired to the mains, I had lost control, let go of the reigns

From that day forward life was never the same, it was struggle after struggle as I lost the game

I had my heroes, John Lennon and Che, Elvis, Mandela, Bob Marley and JFK

But they were rich in spirit and their souls complete, with their achievements I could hardly compete

As I look in the mirror it seems such a shameful waste, a journey taken in too much haste

Blighted by drugs, hubris and greed, and so many things I did not need

At some point or another around the track, perhaps from birth, I was only able to see black

It rendered me weak, far from whole, for I lived me life with a hole in my soul.

That year was relatively calm. I was very depressed but managed to achieve two significant things.

I penned Hole in my Soul and I did some voluntary work for a great charity, MERU that provide assistive technology for severely disabled children.

I settled into a flow of inactivity: Shopping, eating, having a coffee and a couple of cigarettes at a local café and watching TV.

Towards the end of the year I started to get horrendous pains again in my gut. I saw a specialist at St Helier and he confirmed that I had again got a bowel stricture. I needed surgery and that was to be one of three major challenges that awaited me as 2007 became 2008.

Chapter 30

The first challenge was yet another very painful operation. I arrived at Epsom Hospital in February and got prepped for the surgery. Just as I was going to be taken down a message came through that the operation had to be aborted because there was not an Intensive Care bed available post-op.

I went home a mixture of frustration, pain and relief.

The operation did happen a few weeks later but because of the previous problem I had it done at St Anthony's which is a nun run private hospital. The operation was a success and the surgeon said that he had spent most of the three hours that I was under clearing up lesions. When I came round my mum was sitting next to my bed. It was very reassuring. Recovery again was very painful and took some time. I spent a few weeks at my parent's house before returning to Carshalton.

The second challenge had been a bone of contention for five years. My debt mountain which had grown to circa £150,000 was still plaguing me. I was constantly bombarded with demands and I decided after chatting with Jeremy Martell to declare myself bankrupt.

I went to the Citizens Advice Bureau and they were simply brilliant. They took me through all the paper work and helped me list all my creditors. I was declared bankrupt in May and a big weight lifted off my shoulders. Apart from a couple of small personal debts the vast majority of the money was owed to institutions that never should have extended the level of credit in the first place.

In the Summer I went high again. In a desperate attempt to lift my mood I had stopped taking my medication and the consequences were yet again truly awful.

This time I became convinced again that I was a super-agent charged with the responsibility of saving the world. Bizarrely I thought I was being managed and watched and supported by Victoria Beckham.

In a similar way to a schizophrenic hears a voice I was guided by a breeze and followed it's every move. If I felt a breeze on the left hand side of my face I would turn left. In the flat above mine was a guy called Vic and I became convinced that Victoria was talking to me through him.

I was also certain that she was going to visit me in Carshalton and I did a sweep of the High Street in the same fashion to the Grand Hotel. It was after the Rebecca Loos alleged affair and I thought that Victoria was really separated from David.

It was a crazy few weeks. I didn't have any cash so there were no drink, drugs or escorts involved but I did do some very strange things. I talked to people who were on mobile phones and asked them if they were on the phone to my boss. I would wash myself in Carshalton Ponds. I let some homeless people stay in my flat.

One day I went into a nature reserve and went swimming naked in seven different places in the River Wandle. I was washing Simone out of my system so that I was ready for Victoria. Crazy but true.

A dog walker called the police and I was taken to St Helier to be checked out. After I was given the all clear the doctor wanted me to wait for the psychiatrist but I walked out and guided by the breeze went on a rampage of Morden. I would go into gardens and take washing off the line and get changed.

Eventually I ended up in the garden of a house and an enormous German guy confronted me. I told him I was looking for Simone and he replied that was the wrong name. I told him about my book which he looked up on the internet. Having realised that I had a mental illness he called a taxi and gave the driver the fare to take me home.

This carried on until my mum got my GP to visit me and between my mum, the GP and Fiona a sectioning team came round to visit me. I was sectioned again and taken to the Jasper Ward at Sutton Hospital.

I was incensed and created a distraction in my room by smashing my window time and time again against the external protective mesh so much that it came off and went crashing to the floor. While the staff rushed to my room I rushed to the fire exit and put my shoulder hard against the door and it gave way. I was off and went back to the flat barefoot. It was about two miles.

I kicked the door in as I did not have any keys and jumped in the shower. A few minutes later the police arrived and took me back to the hospital.

With my room in Jasper Ward out of commission I was placed in a room on the ground floor. This time I went into the garden and managed to get over one fence and under another and again headed home. If I had any money or credit cards I would have gone to a hotel. I also thought that at any time Victoria would pick me up.

This time at the flat I had to kick down the security device the police had put on the door. Yet again they arrived and instead of taking me back to Sutton Hospital I was taken to a high security unit at Tolworth.

There was no easy exit from this place. There was a twenty foot concrete perimeter wall and several security doors between the ward and the world. I was told the only way out was if there was a fire.

I set my room on fire.

Chapter 31

Sadly the main doors did not open. Even if the doors had have opened where would I have gone anyway. I spent the night in the slammer and another three or four weeks in Tolworth before I was considered safe to return to Jasper ward.

The next eight to twelve months followed the same pattern as before. I was chronically depressed and put on anti-depressants, anti-psychotics and mood stabilisers. I went back to my routine in Carshalton and did what I could to help MERU.

I also helped a couple of talented designers, David and Hayley from Such and Such Design. Their mission was to bring excellent design to disability products and they were highly committed in their endeavours.

In the autumn of 2009 Sam came to live with me. He was depressed himself and a couple of years earlier had moved out to Cyprus with Kim, Phil and Joe. From what I could understand he had a drink and drug problem and wanted to come to me to try and get his life back on track.

I picked him up from Gatwick and he was as pissed as a rat. He was barely able to walk. Thankfully Fiona had driven to East Croydon to pick us up and take us back to Carshalton. I could immediately see the scale of the problem and the task ahead. I worried about whether I had the skills to help him.

The first thing I did with Sam was get him to see the GP. I needed a rapid referral to the mental health team at Sutton hospital. I also needed a sick note because I needed him to claim benefits as I was unable to support both of us on mine.

Sam was diagnosed with anxiety and depression and put on medication. The two of us joined Westcroft Gym and tried to live as healthy a life as possible.

Just before Christmas of 2009 my upstairs neighbour died and John Eggleton came over to clear out and renovate the flat. Sam helped John and did a good job of decorating whilst John replaced the kitchen.

On New Year's Eve I said to John that I was a bit worried about Jane who lived opposite me on the ground floor. I had not seen her for about four or five weeks. He said that he had keys and that he would like me with him when he entered the property.

We opened the door and lying naked in front of us on the floor was Jane. John immediately called the emergency services. It turned out that she had killed herself –one of the brave ones – and had been dead for five weeks. It shocked us all.

I felt that I should have raised the alarm sooner. I didn't because the previous December she had been away at a mother and baby unit. Jane had sadly had her baby removed from her in the middle of 2008 as she was neglecting him. She was fighting to get him back and went to the mother and baby unit to demonstrate her suitability. One night before he was taken away she tried to get me to have him around midnight one evening. She was clearly drunk or drugged because she kept saying that he was my son.

I refused to look after him and she went out in the middle of the night with little James in his push chair. She got picked up in Carshalton High Street and James was taken into temporary foster care. She blamed me for what happened.

For the most part Sam stayed off alcohol but on occasions he would go out and come back paralytic. When he got back after these drinking bouts he would often be very aggressive with me, mostly verbally, and after one such incident that spring I told him it would have to be the last and that I could not cope with it anymore. I was getting worried about the effect it was having on my own mental health and if I ended back up in hospital he would not have been able to stay any longer.

I wanted to get him some Cognitive Behavioural Therapy and I was able to afford to do so in the spring of 2010 when I took a lump sum of about £12,000 from one of my pensions. Sam seemed to enjoy the sessions but I think that he doubted the benefit of them.

Sadly another drinking bout did follow and Sam moved to his grandparents in Virginia Water. I hated not being able to help Sam back to health but it was beyond my capability and as the next few months showed the stress had kicked started another manic episode.

I had become aware of a design company moving into an old bathroom shop in the village and they had converted the front of the shop into a gallery to use as a creative space. It was a beautiful building with double fronted glass picture windows and high ceilings. I was interested in what could be achieved in the space.

Armed with some money in the bank and feeling a little more energised I also wanted to try and re- launch my consultancy career and wanted to explore a new identity. I made with contact with Andrew Candy and his partner Jo Lovelace and arranged to go to a drinks party and networking event that they were hosting.

In no time I put together a show called, rather cheesily, Carshalton's Got Talent that would showcase local art talent. I had met a number of artists at the drinks event and felt that I had enough to put on a good show.

The deal was simple. The artists would each pay a small fixed fee to Andy and Jo for the wall space and I would take 10% of the sales. With most galleries taking 30% to 40% the artists were delighted. The show was a great success and everyone was happy.

At the same time I had Andy working on my corporate identity and in return for about five grand he was putting together the whole package of name, visuals, website and stationary.

Following the success of the first show I put on another one which I called Into the Light. I was back in touch with Julie Pigott at the time and was going to make her the star attraction. I bought about six of her paintings at on average £500 each to help her finance the show. I created a lot of theatre and pulled in good traffic. This show too was a great success, even better than the first. One very talented artist, Gwen Fulton sold three paintings with an average ticket price of about £700.

I really enjoyed playing the impresario and people said that I was like a lightning rod. What could possibly go wrong?

Chapter 32

I went high again.

The gallery attracted a lot of women and I got friendly with Sonia. I spent increasing amounts of time taking her shopping and chilling in the flat. I used a regular driver for a local taxi company who used to ferry us where ever we wanted to go. I got intoxicated with Sonia and it sent me up.

Once again I was a super human figure and Victoria Beckham came back into my thoughts and deeds.

One morning I heard my neighbour Steve and his cousin come in during the early hours and I told them I needed protection. I would pay them to be my bodyguards. That day Sonia and I were going shopping and I had asked Steve to ride with us in the car and do what bodyguards do. He was hopeless and not up to my exacting standards!

At lunchtime I cancelled the arrangement with him and his cousin. I had already paid them both and I asked his cousin for a refund. He proceeded to tell me that he was good at what he did and if I needed any heavy handed work that he was the guy. He refused to return my money and threatened to kill me.

That night I stayed in the Greyhound hotel in Carshalton and the following day the driver took me to the Croydon Park Hotel. I had my head shaven in a dodgy barbers in West Croydon and went shopping for changes of clothes. I was following the breeze again.

The next day I got a train to Brighton and on the train got changed in the toilet and ditched the clothes that I had been wearing in the bin. I also ditched my passport, my mobile phone and my watch. I was convinced the Establishment was after me again and would have trackers in my old clothes and shoes and would be able through electronic surveillance trace the signal from my phone and from the chip on my passport. I was Jason Bourne again – I was on the run.

When I got to Brighton I went and did some pottery painting. I painted a plate for Victoria and told the assistant that it was for Victoria Beckham. I then walked to Hove guided by the breeze and thinking Victoria was watching over me on CCTV. I had lunch in a great burger bar and then went for a massage.

Later I did a tour of the charity shops and in each of them had a complete top to toe change of outfits. I bought a SIM only phone and moved silkily and stealthily about making sure I wasn't being followed.

I got it into my head that Victoria would pick me up at Shoreham Airport so later in the afternoon got the bus over there. I had a few drinks in a pub waiting expectantly for a limo to pull up to collect me. When nothing happened I decided to follow the breeze again and it took me to a small industrial estate where I ditched my money, cheque book and all my belongings except the track suit I got in the last charity shop into a skip.

The breeze took me to a large out of town shopping complex. By now it was dark and raining and I decided to sleep in the woods that surrounded the car park. The wind howled and the rain pelted down. I managed to find some thin plastic sheeting in the dark and wrapped this round me under the track suit. I made a camp from branches and bedded in for a very cold and wet night.

The next morning I emerged from the woods and some builders let me sit in their van for a while and gave me coffee and cigarettes. After they went I visited the large Marks and Spencer and got cleaned up in the toilets. I then went to the coffee shop and downed all the dregs in the discarded cups.

With the breeze still guiding me I went onto the South Downs and eventually found a farm shop. I asked the owner to order me a taxi to take me to Hove via Shoreham. The taxi first took me back to the skip and I managed to retrieve all my belongings and most importantly my money. I was so relieved.

I got a train back to East Croydon and a taxi back to my flat. Reality had dawned. Victoria was not coming for me!

I tried to go back to the gallery but Andy was not interested and asked me to leave. I refused and he got his mobile phone out to call the police. I knocked the phone out of his hand and it broke on the floor. He came at me and I pushed him back across the gallery and crashing into a floor stand. I left.

I felt very dejected after all I had done for Andy at the gallery but in fairness to him I still owed him most of the money for the work he had done for me and I had bounced a cheque on him. He got an order from the Police that excluded me from going near the gallery which they duly delivered.

I was drinking heavily and one night called in an escort. I don't know where my fascination for escorts originates from. It is certainly not just about sex. It is more to do with loneliness.

Searching

My heart beats harder as I await the call, will this be the one standing in the hall

I check through the peephole, see who's outside, invariably beautiful, nothing to hide

I open the door and welcome her in, immediately torn, feeling the sin

I offer a drink, get her to talk, I want to know what makes her walk

A glimmer of light, a smile on the cheek, her heart shines through, mild and meek

The thrill never stops, always a fix, soothing, sublime as our chemicals mix

For her it's a job and normally shows, rarely involved until the action slows

As the end finally comes and it is time to part, off with the skin and back to the start

I wish her good luck and a fond farewell, another encounter for me to dwell.

Fiona and my mum were very worried again. I had cleared out my flat and discarded lots of valuable belongings. They called a sectioning team again who came to visit me with the police one Saturday. As always I was quite plausible and they decided that they could not section me.

On the Sunday I had to go to A and E because my feet were ripped to shreds with all the walking I had been doing. I would not leave the flat because paranoia had set in firmly.

On the Monday and Tuesday I splashed paint all over my flat and finger painted people's names all over the walls. I also built a camp in the little piece of garden at the front of the flat. Fiona phoned me and I said that I was in Camp Bastion.

Simon Russell

Chapter 33

An hour or so later the police arrived and surrounded the flat front and back. The sectioning team asked me if they could come in and anyway they had a court order that allowed them to come into the flat.

This time there was no escape. They could see the paintwork and the camp. They could see the horrendous state of my feet. I barely argued with them. I was exhausted.

By this time the mental health unit at Sutton had been closed and I was taken to Springfield hospital in Tooting.

Incensed yet again that my liberty had been taken away I phoned Fiona and blasted her down the line. I must have made threatening comments because that was the last contact we would have.

I was dressed in shorts and a t-shirt. I discovered that the kitchen had been left open so I went in and got a couple of sharp knives and a stainless steel serving spoon. Armed with these I went into the men's shower room and removed the retainers from the sash windows, hid the knives and bits of wood in the bin and made sure the door was locked and the shower was on. I needed time to get away.

There are two versions about what happened next.

The police believe that I went back to Carshalton, made several vile phone calls to Fiona and set my flat on fire.

My own account is that I spent the night on the common and returned the next morning to find my flat burnt out. I explained to the police that there would be CCTV of me that morning at Tooting Bec station

Either way the flat or all the contents were destroyed and the other five flats had been cleared for safety reasons.

I was taken to Sutton Police Station and left to rest for a while. I was then transported back to Springfield but this time I was placed in the high security Psychiatric Intensive Care Unit (PICU) otherwise known as Ward 1.

When I was finally discharged in December I had nowhere to live and moved into a supported housing project. This was a truly humbling experience. I lived in a large house with seven or eight otherwise homeless men. We each had a small single room and shared the kitchen, lounge and utility room.

The CPS decided that there was insufficient evidence to prosecute me for Arson. However my CRB makes reference to the fire and the belief of the police that I was involved in it.

I moved into my own flat in Sutton in May 2011.

I have not had another manic episode and whilst in a depressed state I have come to realise that this is a far safer place for me and those that I come into contact with.

I have a fabulous doctor, Ewa Zadeh, who has kept me well.

I have managed to write this book which I hope will help other sufferers realise they are not alone. I hope it will also help society in general better understand mental illness.

Apart from writing I Intend to work with companies to ensure they have mentally healthy workplaces.

Sam has recovered well and is now working full time and has his own flat near his mother in West Sussex. We speak two or three times a week and see each other every couple of months or so. I have also developed a good relationship with Joe and he stayed me with me for about six weeks in the summer of 2013.

Finally I am helping to care for my wonderful mother who is currently undergoing treatment for Hodgkins Lymphoma.

A final poem from a new collection I am writing. It is self-explanatory and I hope the subject of my attention gets to read it.

Reunion

Do we look at the same stars?
Is someone joining our dots on Mars?
Are we both moved to tears by the images of war?
Do we both share the same hope for the sick and the poor?
Do we both want to change the verses of the victory song?
Is it in union that our two hearts belong?
Do we both want to share the same life?
Can we be joined together as husband and wife?
Is it our destiny to be together as one?
Oh! My heart aches for that day to come.
These years apart have ripped at my soul
With you by my side I know my soul will be whole

Together we can help change our sickening world
Together our remaining years will be lovingly unfurled
Together we will ride the constant storm
Together we will meet each challenge in whatever form
Our reunion would be the perfect match
And from our painful hibernation we would both hatch.

FIN

Simon Russell